Robinson Public Library District
606 North Jefferson Street
Robinson, IL 62454-2699

The Sad Story of Burton, Speke, and the Nile;

or, Was John Hanning Speke a Cad?

ID0878586

The Sad Story of Burton, Speke, and the Nile; or, Was John Hanning Speke a Cad?

LOOKING AT THE EVIDENCE

W. B. Carnochan

Robinson Public Library District
606 North Jefferson Street
Robinson, IL 62454-2699

STANFORD GENERAL BOOKS

An Imprint of Stanford University Press

Stanford, California 2006

Stanford University Press
Stanford, California
© 2006 by the Board of Trustees of the
Leland Stanford Junior University

No part of this book may be reproduced or transmitted in any form or
by any means, electronic or mechanical, including photocopying and
recording, or in any information storage or retrieval system without
the prior written permission of Stanford University Press.

Library of Congress Cataloging-in-Publication Data

Carnochan, W. B.
    The sad story of Burton, Speke, and the Nile; or, Was John Hanning
Speke a cad? looking at the evidence / W. B. Carnochan.
        p. cm.
    Includes bibliographical references (p.   ) and index.
    ISBN 0-8047-5325-3 (cloth : alk. paper)
    ISBN 0-8047-5571-x (pbk : alk. paper)
    1. Speke, John Hanning, 1827–1864. 2. Burton, Richard Francis, Sir,
1821–1890—Travel—Nile River. 3. Nile River—Discovery and
exploration. 4. Nile River Valley—Discovery and exploration.
5. Explorers—Nile River—History—19th century. I. Title: Sad story
of Burton, Speke, and the Nile. II. Title: Was John Hanning Speke a
cad?. III. Title.
DT117.C37   2006
916.704'23092242—dc22   2005027482

Printed in the United States of America on acid-free, archival-quality
paper

Original Printing 2006
Last figure below indicates year of this printing:
15   14   13   12   11   10   09   08   07   06

Typeset at Stanford University Press in 10/15 Minion

Special discounts for bulk quantities of Stanford General Books
are available to corporations, professional associations, and other
organizations. For details and discount information, contact the
special sales department of Stanford University Press.
Tel: (650) 736-1783, Fax: (650) 736-1784

916.704
Car

FOR MY FRIENDS IN AFRICA

Acknowledgments

Without the generous help of Nicolas Barker, Hugh Bett, Dan Cook, and Michael Smith, new information included in this book about the controversy between Burton and Speke, in particular Speke's account of their parting in Aden in 1859, would not have been available to me. Any book is a collaboration—this one, even more so than some others. Nicolas Barker, always indefatigable, put in hours of concentrated effort on behalf of the project. I am deeply grateful.

I am also grateful to Speke's biographer, Alexander Maitland, who introduced me to the halls of the Royal Geographical Society and shared his expertise; and to Alan Jutzi of the Huntington Library for introducing me to the Huntington's extensive holdings from Burton's library and providing information that I would not otherwise have known.

Dane Kennedy read the manuscript and made helpful suggestions to improve the structure of the whole. He also suggested an important gloss on a central and puzzling question. An observation by Dr. Randall Weingarten, who read the manuscript at a late stage, led to a change of title that usefully clarified the subject matter of the book.

Here at Stanford, my thanks to John Mustain, dogged in his pursuit of material for the Library's collections and hugely helpful; to Eric

Heath, ever patient in answering elementary questions from computer-challenged individuals like myself; to Seth Lerer, a resource for the bibliographical neophyte; and to my old friend Rob Polhemus, who as Chair of the English Department, pried loose funds that eased the burden of research in London at a time when a Starbuck's latte, $3.25 in Palo Alto, cost £3.25 in the United Kingdom, twice as much in dollars. At Stanford University Press, Norris Pope and John Feneron were exemplary editors.

For unstinting encouragement and interest over many years, thanks to Sepp Gumbrecht, Arnold Rampersad, and Ann Schlee.

Finally, my deepest thanks to Brigitte, who in the midst of her own blossoming career as a photographer, manages to be and do many, many other things without which my life would not be remotely the same.

Contents

Chronology

1863   Speke, *Journal of the Discovery of the Source of the Nile.*

1864   Speke, *What Led to the Discovery of the Source of the Nile.*

1864   September 15, Burton and Speke meet at Bath, prior to a debate scheduled on September 16.

1864   September 15, Speke dies of a gunshot wound while shooting near Bath.

1864   December, Burton and James M'Queen, *The Nile Basin.*

1864   Grant, *A Walk across Africa*, dedicated to Speke's memory.

1866   Samuel W. Baker, *The Albert N'yanza: Great Basin of the Nile and Explorations of the Nile Sources.*

1869   John and Kate Petherick, *Travels in Central Africa.*

1872   Burton, "Captain Speke," Chapter 12, Part 2, *Zanzibar.*

1890   October 19, Burton dies in Trieste.

1893   Isabel Burton, *The Life of Captain Sir Richard F. Burton.*

The Sad Story of Burton, Speke, and the Nile; or, Was John Hanning Speke a Cad?

CHAPTER ONE

Introduction

The mid-nineteenth century in Britain was a great age of African exploration. The missionary David Livingstone (1813–1873) and the adventurers Richard Burton (1821–1890) and John Hanning Speke (1827–1864) were public heroes. But the partnership of Burton and Speke, in their legendary search for the source of the Nile, was strained almost from the start of their acquaintance. A climax came after Speke claimed, in 1858, to have discovered the Nile source in the lake he named after Queen Victoria. Burton did not accompany Speke to the lake, for reasons that are less than clear, and he passionately rejected Speke's claim. He also charged him with violating a promise not to report his discovery to the Royal Geographical Society without Burton also being present. The sad ending of their story came in September 1864, following another African expedition by Speke and James Augustus Grant to confirm the Nile source. Speke and Burton were to debate the question of the Nile at a meeting of the British Association for the Advancement of Science in Bath. On the day before the debate, the two met on the platform where it was scheduled to take place. Speke immediately left in agitation without a word to Burton. A few hours later he was dead, dying of a gunshot wound suffered while shooting partridge at his cousin's estate nearby. Burton lived twenty-six more years.

Of the two travellers, Burton has had by far the larger amount of attention. He is so compelling a figure that, in addition to the many biographies, both popular and scholarly, that he has inspired, a website is now devoted to his life and work. Burton's domination of the airwaves, as it were, has had consequences in narratives devoted to him and to Speke. What we think we know has been largely filtered through a Burtonian lens. This book attempts to redress the balance by examining the conflict as it was waged in a series of duelling texts by the protagonists. Though I have made grateful use of archival work by others, I have not otherwise drawn on the rich materials housed in the Royal Geographical Society, the National Library of Scotland, and elsewhere. In a sense, this might even be called a "literary" or at least a textual study, in that way harking back to my earliest training in literature at a time when "close reading" was all the rage. I have tried to read the relevant texts closely–and to see what we learn thereby.

And, if there is a single lesson embodied in the duelling texts, it is that history itself is a battle of competing stories, dependent on inference and intuition, not on the bedrock of some supposedly plain facts. Nothing is new in this lesson, but the countless questions raised by the story of Burton and Speke provide pointed illustration of its basic truth. Although some of the evidence I offer counts in Speke's favor, and though I think history has done him something less than justice, this is less important, in the last analysis, than the tangled skein of historical evidence, illustrated here in a setting that has long evoked strong feelings on one side or the other. Perhaps Speke, as some have thought, was a cad. More likely, as I think, not; or not really. But what is conclusively so: we will not ever know perfectly for sure.

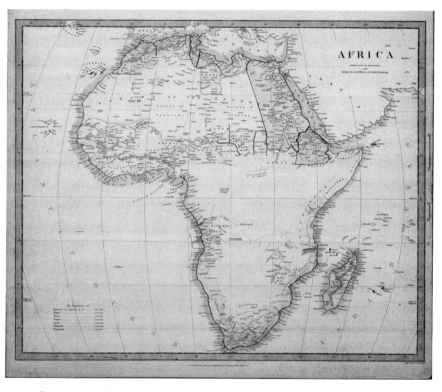

Africa. Engraved by J. and C. Walker. (London, Society for the Diffusion of Useful Knowledge, 1839.) The map shows the unexplored interior of Central Africa as a vast, empty space. Courtesy Department of Special Collections, Stanford University Libraries.

Africa. With the discoveries to May 1858 of Livingstone, Barth, Vogel, and the Chadda expedition from documents in possession of the Royal Geographical Society. Engraved by George Swanston. (Edinburgh, A. Fullarton and Co. 1860?) The first map to show "Lake Victoria," so named by Speke in 1858, as the source of the Nile. Courtesy Department of Special Collections, Stanford University Libraries.

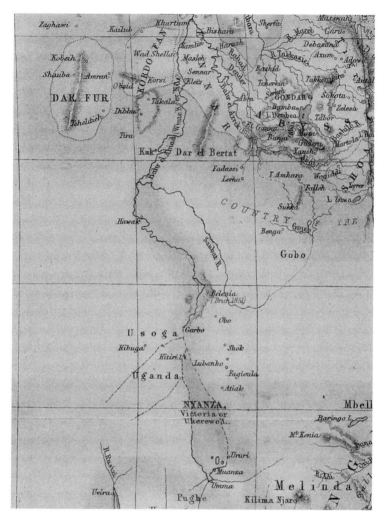

Detail of facing map.

John Hanning Speke. "Engraved by S. Hollyer from a Photograph by South-well Brothers." Frontispiece, John Hanning Speke, *Journal of the Discovery of the Source of the Nile* (Edinburgh and London: W. Blackwood and Sons, 1863). The studio backdrop alludes to Speke's explorations.

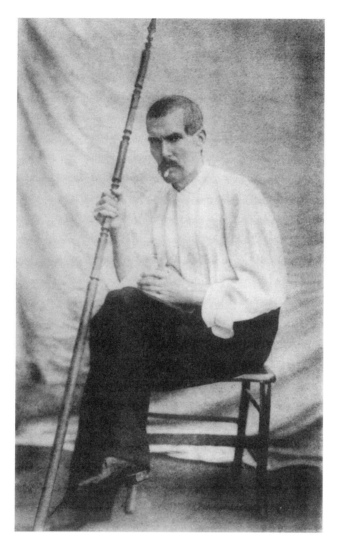

"Richard Burton in his Tent in Africa." Frontispiece, Isabel Burton, *The Life of Captain Sir Richard F. Burton*, ed. W. H. Wilkins (London: Duckworth, 1898).

CHAPTER TWO

The Odd Couple

Sir Richard Francis Burton scarcely needs introduction. A lush romantic figure in the Victorian landscape, he mesmerizes his biographers, including his wife and first biographer Isabel Arundel.[1] He was a soldier, a traveller who went in disguise to the sacred Islamic cities of Mecca, Medina and Harar, a connoisseur of erotica and sexual practices, the author and translator of countless books, a proto-anthropologist, a linguist, a poet (though not a good one[2])—and an enigma. Fawn Brodie takes the title of her biography, *The Devil Drives* (1967), from Burton's answer to his own question, why suffer the hardships and risks of adventuring? Mary S. Lovell's *A Rage to Live* (1998) recalls the tangled contradictions of a (female) character in Pope's "Epistle to a Lady": "[You] purchase pain with all that joy can give,/ And die of nothing but a rage to live."

Throughout Burton's story runs the thread of mystery. What, exactly, did the journals and diaries contain that Isabel burned so conscientiously after his death? What to make of his sexuality: homoerotic, homosexual, heterosexual, bisexual, voyeurist, pederastic, omnivorous? Or of his masquerades as an Arab: just a way of gaining access to a forbidden world (which they were) or, psychologically construed, flagrant cross-dressing? They struck his fellow explorer John Hanning Speke, whose name and story are intimately and irrevocably linked with his, as below the dignity of an English officer, and Speke took pains to report that the natives of Somaliland "consider the Arab's gown and trousers effeminate." [3]

Finally, there are Burton's often vexed dealings with others, especially with Speke. Did Speke in fact "betray" Burton by telling him he would not report the discovery of the source of the Nile to the Royal Geographical Society until Burton, still in Aden, could join him in London—and then doing what he had promised not to do? Burton's biographers assume, on his authority, that this is so, and Speke's biographer Alexander Maitland does not essentially doubt it, though he is on the lookout for extenuating circumstances, including the influence of others. No matter how often the story of Burton and Speke has been told, uncertainties linger. My aim is not to dispel them—though I would if I could—but to ferret out where in the evidence, of which there is a great deal, they lie. Truth, or call it "truth," lurks in the shadows.

An odder couple than Burton and Speke could hardly be found. Alan Moorehead, in his chronicle of the search for the White Nile, calls their partnership "as ironic a phenomenon as anything Cervantes contrived with his Don Quixote and Sancho Panza." But Quixote and Sancho Panza were able to love each other, while the partnership between Burton and Speke turned into mutual recrimination and hatred. It seems a dark joke of fate that threw them together on their journeys, first to Somaliland and then, looking for the Nile, to the lake regions of central Africa. Unlike the exotic and un-English-seeming Burton (though he was born in Devon, the son of a colonel who hoped he would become a clergyman and the grandson of a well-to-do country gentleman), Speke was about as English as it was possible to be, coming from an old family that had lived for generations in rural Somerset, that most squirearchical of counties in the West country. Burton was the more gregarious of the two, notwithstanding his abrasive relationships with others, especially his superiors. Speke was a loner who loved shooting birds and animals and, while in the Indian army, sought out remote parts of the Himalayas in search of ever more game to kill; "there are . . . but few animals" (he wrote with no little glee) "to be found in either India, Tibet, or the Himalaya Mountains, specimens of which have not fallen victims to my gun." Burton, on the other hand, could not have been less drawn to the culture of sport and of the gun, and he joked about Speke's sporting habits: not having had the luck to "distinguish himself" in action while with the Indian Army, says Burton, Speke "applied himself, with his wonted energy, to make war upon the fauna and ferae of the Himalayas." Isabel Burton claimed that Burton had known twenty-nine languages; Speke had to get along almost entirely in English, a limitation that made considerable difficulty for him in Somaliland and that Burton regarded as a mark of lesser talents. Burton, whatever his sexual tastes, unquestionably had plenty of them; Speke, who never married, seems to have had modest interest at most either in women or in men. For all that, the two had much in common. Each yearned for adventure and fame. Each was ambitious, if in different ways. Each was exceedingly brave and very hardy.[4]

Evidence of what happened between them, beginning with their expedition to Somaliland in 1855, is plentiful, almost all of it embedded in their own differing accounts—that is, in the numerous printed texts on which I substantially rely. Among the major sources are: 1) Burton's *First Footsteps in East Africa* (1856), in which he printed as an appendix, with drastic amendment, Speke's journal of their first voyage; 2) Speke's narrative, in part based on the same journal that Burton had abridged and in part on his own earlier publications in *Blackwood's*, *What Led to the Discovery of the Source of the Nile* (1864)—his account, first of joining up with Burton in Aden, then of events in Somaliland, and then, during the voyage to the lake regions, of striking out by himself to seek the source of the Nile; 3) Burton's *The Lake Regions of Central Africa* (1860); 4) segments of Burton's journal and writings describing what happened in the expedition to the lakes, including Speke's farewell to him in Aden and events just prior to Speke's strange death in 1864, all printed by Isabel Burton in her hero-worshipping biography (1893); and 5) the chapter that Burton called "Captain Speke" and appended to the second volume of his *Zanzibar* (1872), a narrative otherwise completed more than a decade before its publication. The preponderance of evidence, that is to say, comes from Burton and his writings, though not all of it.

What has long been missing and only recently found, under unusual circumstances, is Speke's own account of his farewell to Burton, as the second expedition ended; nor does he anywhere allude directly to the quarrel that ensued when, in Burton's telling, Speke violated his promise not to report his findings to the Royal Geographical Society except in Burton's company. Much depends on what can be inferred, or not, from matters glossed over or explained only in a fragmentary way. There will always be some who love Burton and others who defend Speke even if they do not love him. The story of these two extraordinary men, with its sorry end in Speke's self-inflicted though probably accidental gunshot wound on the day before they were to debate the great question of the Nile, is an object lesson in the trickiness of sorting and adjudicating historical evidence, in this case evidence known to us through the printed word.

CHAPTER THREE

The Story Begins: Aden

It was accident that brought the two men together. The bone-dry port of Aden, taken over by the British in 1839, used as a fueling stop for ships on their way to or from India and known as the "coal hole" of the East, also became a gateway to East Africa. In the autumn of 1854, Burton was waiting in Aden for permission from the East India Company to mount an expedition to Somaliland, hoping first to traverse the country to Harar in Abyssinia and then to explore the interior of Somaliland. The journey to Harar, potentially full of risk, was the sort that Burton had made his specialty by venturing to Mecca and Medina. The exploration of Somaliland itself, had it been successful, would have been the ordinary combination of adventuring and pre-colonial prospecting for territorial advantage. Burton found he was opposed, however, by Colonel James Outram, recently appointed as Political Resident in Aden. Outram was the type of Indian Army bureaucrat whom Speke got along with well—and Burton did not.

Outram felt that Somaliland was too dangerous a place for any of his officers to go exploring; or that is the explanation he gave Burton. Alexander Maitland thinks Outram may have had other motives, including his dislike of Burton's former commanding officer in India, Sir Charles Napier, who would have received Burton's report of his notorious investigation of male brothels in Karachi.[1] Perhaps Outram also mis-

trusted Burton, as many did, by reason of his arrogance, his un-regi-
mental ways, and the hint of sexual scandal that he bore with him.
Lovell, to the contrary, thinks Outram's opposition to the Somali expedition, which contrasted with his own younger hopes of exploring
Somaliland (or so Burton claimed) and with his earlier support for Burton's proposals, stemmed from "genuine concern." And, probably con-
firming Lovell's opinion, when the young John Hanning Speke, on leave
from the Indian army, twenty-seven years old and Burton's junior by six
years, arrived in Aden, hoping to hunt game in Somaliland, Outram
objected no less to his plans than to Burton's, and on the same grounds.
Maitland imagines what finally happened: Speke "continued to pester
Outram, showering him with sweet words and entreaties, until in the
end the Resident weakened sufficiently to palm his tireless opponent off
on Richard Burton." Outram would serve as Political Resident in Aden
only briefly. Perhaps he decided it was not worth his trouble to oppose
the determined adventurers.[2]

What do we learn from the protagonists? For Speke, Outram is a
man of "frank and characteristic ardour"; his reluctance to allow an expedition to Somaliland, that of a benevolent Christian who does not
wish others to hazard their lives—but even in Speke's account Outram's
benevolence is self-regarding: "After repeated supplications on my part,
the generous kind nature of the Colonel overcame him, and he thought
of a pretext by which, should anything serious happen to me, there
would not remain any onus on his conscience." Cohabiting with Outram's generosity and kindness is also the "pretext"—that of putting
Burton in charge of Speke's fate—by which he hopes to absolve himself
of responsibility for any bad results that might befall the expedition.
Speke is not a sophisticated writer or thinker, and he is not bothered by
what we would think of as ethical duplicity. Instead we see Outram
through admiring eyes. The dedication to *What Led to the Discovery of
the Source of the Nile* reads: "To the memory of Lieut.-General Sir James
Outram . . . who first gave me a start in Africa." Whether it was Outram

or Burton who could best be described as having given Speke his start in Africa is a fair question.[3]

Burton's account of these events in "Captain Speke" is oblique, quite different from Speke's, more subtle, sometimes more obscure—and also composed at a greater remove of time, with whatever consequences that may have entailed. The accounts diverge from the very moment Speke sets foot in Aden. In Burton's story, it is Speke's naivete that leads him to bring cheap goods for barter that "the simple-minded negroes of Africa"—Burton takes that phrase from *What Led . . .*, with an implication of his own superior acumen—would in fact "have rejected with disdain." Speke also displays his inexperience by signing on the first Somalis he meets, mere "donkey-boys" who speak no English, "to become his Abbans—guides and protectors." We hear no more of these donkey-boys, but they are not the guides Sumunter and Ahmed, engaged by Burton "to assist me" in Speke's account, guides who were to give him a great deal of difficulty.[4]

The questions raised by the differing accounts are: who was the better judge of character; and who bore responsibility for Speke's failed mission to the Nogal Valley in Somaliland while Burton was on his dashing, daring visit to Harar? Accusing Speke of bad judgment in hiring his donkey-boys, Burton seems to parry the other's claim that he, Burton, erred in hiring Sumunter and Ahmed, and even that he may have wished Speke ill from the start, to the point of hoping to undermine him. Sumunter and Ahmed were of the same tribe, the Warsingali, and spoke the same language. "This," Speke writes in a peevish footnote, "proved a great mistake. By having both men of the same tribe for my entire dependence, they invariably acted in concert against me like two brothers." Why the two should invariably act in concert is not obvious unless one assumes either the native rascality of all Warsingali tribesmen or malice aforethought on Burton's part. But suspicions about Burton's intentions toward Speke are probably not warranted. It was, after all, very early in their acquaintance.[5]

As for Colonel Outram, Burton uses Speke's praise, which Burton thinks quite misguided, as his starting point: "I applied officially to the Political Resident of Aden, the late Colonel, afterwards Sir James, Outram, of whose 'generous kind nature' and of whose 'frank and characteristic ardour' my personal experience do [sic] not permit me to speak with certainty." His "personal" inability "to speak with certainty" leaves no doubt that Burton was far from sharing Speke's estimate of Outram's character. And when he comes to Outram's role, and his own, in Speke's joining the Somaliland expedition, he is careful to insist, though obliquely, on his own position of command and to dispute the benign reading of Outram's motives. "Upon my assuming the fullest responsibility and giving a written bond for our blood, the Political Resident allowed me to enroll Lieut. Speke as a member of the Expedition." In this version, however laced with sarcasm, it is not a matter of Outram asking Burton, or telling him, to sign on Speke but permitting him to do so. And Burton finds Outram's attempt to salve his conscience distasteful: "Colonel Outram would also have gratified his own generosity, and shifted all onus from his conscience, by making me alone answerable for the safety of a Madras officer who had left India expressly to join us." Though the ungenerous nature of Outram's generosity is indisputable, the description of Speke as having left India "expressly to join us" might slip by unnoticed. He did not come to Aden expressly to join the expedition but to hunt game in Africa, as Burton himself has already reported. He is letting his reader know, again, who is in charge, always a point of contention and abraded feelings for Speke, who sometimes intimated that he was the fitter leader and that, on their subsequent expedition to the lakes, Burton was only nominally in command. In Burton's well-wrought prose are the lineaments of the power struggle to come. What he presents is not exactly the whole truth he had promised. [6]

The sentence that follows is more obscure: "I had, however, now done enough: common report at Aden declared the thing to be impossible, and the unfortunate traveller returned unsuccessful." What is the thing that was declared impossible? Burton appears to be saying that taking on sole responsibility for Speke's safety was more than he could promise, or should have to, that everyone ("common report") agreed with him, and that Speke, if he is the unfortunate traveller, returned to Outram (perhaps) with the news that Burton would not accept Outram's terms. Possibly Burton alludes to Thomas Nashe's *The Unfortunate Traveller* (1594) and its picaresque hero Jacke Wilton, one of whose pranks was passing himself off as the Earl of Surrey (recalling Speke's self-image as a more suitable and effective leader than Burton). Is Burton associating himself with the tolerant Earl who ultimately forgives Jacke Wilton his transgression?[7] That is not out of the question, considering Burton's learning, his sly ways, and his pleasure in concealment and disguise.[8]

This unexpected recruit to Burton's party was, for its leader, a puzzle and a problem from the start: "Lieut. Speke was uncommonly hard to manage." No doubt, on the one hand, he was hard to manage; yet, on the other, Burton is making sure, once again, that the reader knows who was the manager and who, the managed. "Having been for years his own master"—Burton is thinking of Speke's solitary pursuit of game— "he had a way as well as a will of his own. To a peculiarly quiet and modest aspect—aided by blue eyes and blonde hair" (Burton was dark-haired and dark-eyed)—"to a gentleness of demeanour" (Burton was not gentle in his demeanor; to some he looked like Satan), "and an almost childlike simplicity of manner which at once attracted attention" (Burton attracted attention for quite different traits), "he united an immense and abnormal fund of self-esteem, so carefully concealed, however, that none but his intimates suspected its existence." In the outcome, the master of disguise who penetrated the closed world of Harar thinks he has been misled by the deceptively plain-spoken, plain-looking, plain-seeming, childishly simple Englishman who turned up in Aden looking for sport and for adventure. [9]

Now there comes a moment of almost eerie strangeness: "Before we set out [Speke] openly declared that being tired of life he had come to be killed in Africa." "Not," says Burton crankily, "a satisfactory announcement to those"—himself—"who aspired to something better than the crown of martyrdom." Speke's utterance is almost certainly authentic, if not necessarily exact. Perhaps he did not say that he came to be "killed" in Africa but that he came to "die." But only if you believe Burton to have been capable of almost any fiction—in this case, of attributing to Speke a desire to die so as to avert the belief that the quarrel with Burton killed him—is it possible to believe Speke said absolutely nothing of the kind.[10]

Could he have been in some way joking? "See Africa and die?" Or was this blond and blue-eyed Englishman afflicted with private demons? In fact Burton came to believe that Speke later suffered mental damage, the result of an illness while on their journey to the lake regions, but here he dismisses the idea because, "when the opportunity came he behaved with prudence as well as courage." Instead, Speke's talk of coming to Africa to be killed must have been "whimsical affectation," like his habit of employing a kind of "broken English" when he returned home, "as if he had forgotten his vernacular in the presence of strange tongues." But saying that one is coming to Africa to be killed or even to die does not much resemble an innocent eccentricity of speech and manner. Maitland explains what Speke said as "somewhat Byronic . . . fatalism," but fatalism, even if Speke is alluding (as Maitland believes) to his dangerous quest for dangerous game, is one thing; coming to Africa tired of life and looking for death is another. Learning that Speke had died of his gunshot wound in 1864, Burton supposed it was suicide, not a grievous accident. He must have had vividly in mind whatever it was Speke said to him, years before, about having come to Africa to be killed. That is (after all) what in a sense did happen, though at a later time and in a different country.[11]

CHAPTER FOUR

Somaliland

The seeds of trouble were sown, first, as a consequence of Speke's inability to carry out the mission Burton assigned him, possibly just to keep him occupied while Burton travelled to Harar—that of locating the Wadi Nogal, a river in the Nogal Valley that earlier explorers had identified in the 1840's.[1] Then, far more seriously, a Somali attack at the outset of their attempt to launch a major expedition into the interior not only inflicted serious damage on their party, ending the expedition before it began, but engendered in Speke deep resentment, for he thought Burton, in the midst of the combat, had questioned his skill and resolution as a soldier.

Speke's frustration at failing to locate the Wadi Nogal was intensified by the scandalous behavior of his abban, Sumunter, whom Burton had hired. And, after the events in Somaliland, Burton further offended Speke by printing an adapted version of his Somali journal in *First Footsteps* (as Speke supposed, wrongly, to Burton's profit) and by commandeering biological specimens that Speke had gathered, intending them for a collection at "Jordans," his family home in Somerset. As commander of the expedition, Burton had good claim to the journal and to the specimens, but the ever-growing contest for predominance between the two men colored what could otherwise have been accepted as merely routine circumstance.

Still they might have managed to get on successfully enough, if not for what happened during the fierce skirmish at Berbera in April, 1855, between native tribesmen and Burton's "little party" of "forty-two souls"—officers, armed recruits, private servants—that ended with Burton and Speke seriously wounded and one of their fellow officers dead. Why the engagement happened at all was a serious question: did Burton, as some thought, bear responsibility? But the still larger question, especially in Speke's mind, was: who behaved better under battle conditions? It was essential to both their interests to come off as quicker on the draw, more reliable, the better fighter. Without the episode at Berbera, things might not have turned out so disastrously as they did in the long run.[2]

The Wadi Nogal

The two separate parts of *What Led to the Discovery of the Source of the Nile* (1864) came out originally, in different form, in issues of *Blackwood's Edinburgh Magazine* during autumn, 1859, and early summer, 1860. The installments in *Blackwood's* appeared in reverse chronological order, the expedition to the lakes preceding that to Somaliland. The expedition to the lakes took precedence because it provided the basis of Speke's claim to the Nile, which made him a hot property and one Blackwood's badly wanted for its own. Publishing the Somali story thereafter meant capitalizing further on the firm's investment. For Speke it meant a chance to give his own version of the story that Burton had edited in *First Footsteps*. The Somali journal had become publishable, as it would not so readily have been before Speke had claimed the Nile.

Now Speke had the chance both to profit from his Somali adventures and to revise what he wrote originally—with one eye on Burton's edit-

ing job. The extent to which Speke reworked his original is beyond re-
capture, because it has not been found, but we can be sure that the story
of his unsuccessful effort, acting on Burton's instructions, to locate the
Wadi Nogal has had the benefit of some revision. We also know, on
Speke's authority, that his "Adventures in Somali Land" are not taken
from his journal alone: "I must explain that I never kept diaries with a
view to publishing what I wrote . . . . Further I would add, I have been
obliged to extract nearly as much matter from letters which I wrote to
my mother, and which have all been sedulously kept, as from the diaries
themselves." Speke's Somali narrative, as we find it in *Blackwood's* and in
the similar but not identical version in *What Led . . .* , is a tangled composite, the sort of text we have come to recognize as normative in its
heterogeneity. "Lieutenant Speke's Diary," as edited by Burton in *First
Footsteps*, and Burton's own account of events, years later, in "Captain
Speke" complicate—some might say, enrich—matters further. In any
case, the clash between the two men plays itself out in intricate precincts
of the written word.[3]

While he resented Burton's authority, Speke also wanted it known
that he was a good soldier who obeyed orders. If he did not locate the
river, it was not for want of trying: "I had many conferences about THE
WADI NOGAL, which Lieut. Burton had desired me to investigate, but
could obtain no satisfactory information. They [Speke's informants]
said there were many wadys in Nogal . . ." In hindsight, however, he believes he can identify the object of his failed search: "at a distance of five
or six marches, there was a nullah"—an intermittent watercourse—
"with many springs in it, which united in certain places, and became a
running stream. This I now, from subsequent inquiries and inspection
of Lieut. Cruttenden's map, suspect is the watercourse set down in my
instructions for the Wady Nogal." Lieutenant Charles Cruttenden of the
Indian Navy had mapped parts of eastern Somaliland in the 1840's, and
Speke uses the mention of his map to lay blame on Burton in a self-ex-
culpatory footnote: "Unfortunately, when sent on this mission, I was

not furnished with a chart, and had never seen any works written on the subject." It was Burton's responsibility, Speke is letting us know, to provide information that would have enabled him to carry out his assignment. Decidedly he has a point, though "unfortunately" is disingenuous and though we can guess at what Burton's answer would have been. More than once he referred to the Wadi Nogal as a "celebrated" feature of the Somali landscape, implying that, since it was celebrated, it should not have been all that hard to find; and that, if Speke had only possessed greater linguistic ability, he could have found it.[4]

When Burton printed his amendment of Speke's journal in *First Footsteps*, he had little knowledge, or none, of Speke's hostile feeelings, and he treats Speke's failed mission to the Wadi Nogal respectfully in his preface: "He had failed, through the rapacity and treachery of his guide, to reach the Wady Nogal. But he had penetrated beyond the maritime chain of hills,"—as others had not—"and his journal . . . proves that he had collected some novel and important information." In his introduction to the journal itself, however, there appears a glimmer of animus as Burton explains again why the mission failed: "The bad conduct of his Abban, and the warlike state of the country, prevented his reaching the 'Wady Nogal,' which, under more favourable circumstances and with more ample leisure than our plans allowed him, he conceives to be a work of little difficulty and no danger." Does Burton admire Speke's insouciant optimism? We are more likely to feel instead that it bespeaks naivete, even granting that the Wadi Nogal is celebrated. Burton after all understood the difficulties and dangers of adventuring—and reveled in them: "Starting in a hollowed log of wood—some thousand miles up a river, with an infinitesimal prospect of returning! I ask myself 'Why?' and the only answer is 'damned fool!' . . . the Devil drives." Even though Burton allows for the difficult circumstances of Speke's mission, and even if we take his view of Speke's optimism as in some degree admiring, the contrast is pronounced between the savvy, seasoned, devil-possessed explorer, on the one hand, and the solid English gentleman out on safari, on the other.[5]

In the retrospective "Captain Speke," after all that had happened between them, Burton turns Speke's failure to locate the Wadi Nogal into
the material of glum comedy: "I returned to Aden on Feb. 9th, 1855, and
was followed about a week afterwards by Lieut. Speke. He was thoroughly disgusted with his journey, and he brought back a doleful tale of
trouble." It is the faintly antique "doleful" that casts a comic gleam.
Speke could be a medieval knight of sorry countenance, undone not
only by time and circumstance but by his own fallibility. And he serves
up excuses for his failure: "He had adopted, by my advice, a kind of half-
eastern dress, as did Colonel Pelly and his officers, when visiting El
Riyaz, the headquarters of the Wahhabis; and he attributed to this cos-
tume all his misfortunes." While Speke, like Outram, did not think well
of English officers dressed as Arabs, it is hard to suppose that he ever attributed "all his misfortunes" to his mode of dress. Burton uses the occasion, possibly trumped up, to vindicate his own advice, and his own
practice, against Speke and Outram, giving the instance of Colonel
(later, Sir) Lewis Pelly, who ordered his officers and servants to "wear
the Abba over their clothes so as to avoid unnecessary annoyance and
thieving" while on a dangerous mission to Riyadh in 1865. None could
claim that Pelly, a model of English colonial authority, was stooping below the dignity or the masculinity of an English officer in adopting
Arab dress.[6]

Although Burton uses Speke's version of the story as a starting point
when dealing with Colonel Outram, now he looks away from his rival's
account or perhaps decides to rely altogether on his own memory:
Speke "came back," Burton writes, "determined that no such feature as
the Wady Nogal existed." This is a radical reconstruction both of Speke's
story and Burton's own as it had appeared in *First Footsteps*. Yet the
claim—like the report of Speke's coming to Africa "to be killed"—may
be based in fact, even if spun to Burton's advantage. Perhaps he is exag-
gerating Speke's report that his informants told him there were many
wadis in Nogal and that he could not obtain satisfactory information.
Perhaps he is remembering extravagant words—one can imagine Speke

exclaiming, "there's no such thing as the bloody Wadi Nogal"—uttered in frustration. But to the extent that there is a basis to Burton's story, Speke's opposing version represents salvage work on behalf of his reputation. Having claimed the Nile, he had good reason to present himself as a careful geographer who could make sense of Somali geography when he saw Cruttenden's map, and whose failure to locate the Wadi Nogal was not his fault but Burton's (in not providing him with information and not hiring a competent guide). Whatever the true story, *amour-propre* drives the contest.[7]

Sumunter

Another power struggle, one from which Speke may have learned something about his liabilities in such a contest, was with his cagy, unreliable abban, Sumunter—or Samater, as the name is spelled in the *Blackwood*'s text. In the eventual outcome, Sumunter's conviction and punishment in Aden for malfeasance, other differences between Speke and Burton broke into the open. Speke's troubles with his abban play no more than a small part in the journal as Burton printed it in *First Footsteps* nor do they play any part in "Captain Speke." As a result, it is necessary to rely on Speke, and what he tells us is often very odd. A neophyte in African exploration when he was in Somaliland, he faced a dilemma in describing his travails with Sumunter: on the one hand, he wants to persuade us, since the abban was Burton's choice, that the fault lay there; on the other, he risks seeming an incompetent leader. The dilemma helps account for strains in the narrative and the sense of frustration, amounting even to despair, that eventually colors it. In the twists and turns of his struggles with Sumunter, we catch sight of complications in Speke that coexist with his essential innocence.

Needing money to pay off debts, Sumunter on one occasion makes off with cash given him to hire donkeys, and with salt and cloth from the expedition's store of supplies. A phantasmagoric colonial comedy ensues, as if it came from the imagination of Gilbert and Sullivan, in which Speke enlists the local sultan to hear his grievances and, he hopes, to administer justice. That is not how it works out. Having been accused, in the sultan's presence, of rascally behavior—Speke calls his actions "villainies"—Sumunter "appeared very humble, and denied flatly all the accusations I brought against him." Therefore: "I begged the sultan, flattering him with his great renown for administering justice, that he would do me justice as his guest." The trial that follows is conducted according to some obscure blend of English and Somali custom after Speke and the sultan have reached an accord: the sultan "said he was willing to do anything for me if I would direct the way in which I wished him to proceed; he did not understand English law, and I must submit to Somali methods." On the one hand, the sultan asks for instructions; on the other, he declares the primacy of Somali custom. Speke seems not to understand the contradiction. Wishing to appear in control, he looks more like a character in a colonial farce, almost forfeiting (one would think) whatever credit he may have stored up in the matter of the Wadi Nogal. The trial does nothing to abate the impression of Savoyard foolishness.[8]

The participants arrange themselves for the hearing with the sultan seated on bales of cloth, Speke and his servants sitting together "at the gable end of the tent," and Sumunter facing them. Speke then opens "the proceedings of the prosecution," recording them in dialogue between "P," himself as prosecutor, and "D," Sumunter as defendant. The playlet, which depends on Speke's interpreter, Ahmed, for its very existence, continues for almost two full pages. What follows is roughly the second half of the drama:

P.— "Where are the twenty rupees I gave you for hiring donkeys, and which I particularly ordered should not be expended for any other purpose?

Sumunter, putting his hand fixedly in his breast, said, "I've got them; they are all right. I will give them to you presently."

Speke.— "No! give them to me now; I want them this instant."

Sumunter, confused and fumbling at his pocket, much to the delight of all the court, who burst with laughter, said, "No! I've left them at home in Bunder Gori, and will give them by-and-by."

Judge.— "Ahem!" and the prosecution continued.

P.— "Why did you change my good rice for bad?" (opening and showing the contents of the nearest sack).

D.— "I thought it would not signify: bad rice is good enough for the camel-drivers, and I have left enough good for your consumption. An old friend asked me for it, and I did it to oblige him."

Judge.— "Ahem!" and the prosecution continued.

P.— "Why did you attempt to bribe Farhan to leave my service, and say nothing to me about it?"

D.— "Farhan is a bad man; and I was afraid he would steal your things."

Judge.— "Ahem!"

Thus ended the prosecution and defence.[9]

Since nothing of this trial appears in Burton's printing of "Lieutenant Speke's Diary," we might guess that Speke composed the drama to entertain his mother. In any case, as with any reconstruction of dialogue and action, and even leaving aside the interpreter's role, we have to wonder how near it comes to reality. No avatar of Colonel Blimp could have managed it better. The sultan's intermittent "ahems!" are comic triumphs, whether or not Speke recognizes them for what they are, and the struggle between English officer and Somali rascal may leave a reader on the side of Sumunter and rascality.

In the outcome, the judicial comedy intended to display English fair play turns into tragi-comic farce, and Speke is a sorry loser in this colonial game of wits: "The sultan raised his head, and in answer to my appeal as to what judgment he would give, calmly said, he could see no harm in what had been done—Sumunter was my Abban, and, in virtue of the ship he commanded, was at liberty to do whatever he pleased either with or to my property." The wonder is that Speke allows himself, not to mention the British empire, thus to be abased in public view. It is as if he courted humiliation. (And could the sultan possibly have spoken of Sumunter as a ship's commander?) The sultan's words, Speke writes, are "equivalent to saying I had come into a land of robbers, and therefore must submit to being robbed; and this I plainly told him." Only after he says he wants to return to Aden rather than stay in a country whose sultan is less powerful than Sumunter does Speke regain the upper hand.[10]

Mixing assertion and passivity, his self-representation leaves us in some shock. His continuing travails with Sumunter, who becomes more and more obstructionist, refusing to follow orders and hiding out with his family to avoid travelling into the territory of his enemies, are those of a colonial innocent at bay: "I daily tried to draw Sumunter, like a badger, from his hut, which was four miles distant from my tent, but without effect. He and his wife, two dwarf sisters (little bits of things, who, the interpreter said, were too small to be of any use), and some children, all lived together in a small beehive hut, so low that they had to crawl in on all-fours, and so small that it was marvellous how they could turn round in it." Baffled and outfoxed, Speke regards the lot of them as barely human.[11]

On January 3, 1855—six weeks before the party returned to Aden—Sumunter finally turns up, surly as ever: "At length to-day he arrived in a sullen angry mood, and said, haughtily, he was displeased at my trying to force him into compliance, as if I had the power to make him move unless he chose." This throws Speke into a rage: "It was impossible to keep one's temper under such constant provocation; so I abused him vehemently, . . . and entreated he would 'get away,' and let me take my chance of proceeding how I could, for his presence simply made my position one of purgatory. He laughed in scorn. . . ." Speke and his abban resemble partners in a bad marriage: one always trying, or seemingly trying, to get rid of the other until they eventually regroup, only to go on suffering together. But it is Speke's telling Sumunter, whether it actually happened at the time or only in the recounting, that he is in "purgatory" that colors the account with something like desperation. Neither Sumunter nor any interpreter would be likely to have attached any sensible meaning to the idea of purgatory. The sense of affliction may be set beside, for contrast, the initial, insouciant confidence Burton attributes to Speke and, as well, the self-humiliating yet comic trial he had sponsored less then two months before. Despite it all, and still in the manner of a bad marriage, Sumunter returns with Speke to Aden, where the expedition is to be reconstituted.[12]

Approaching the sea, Speke recovers his spirits, as at the lifting of a great burden: "The inexpressible delight I felt at snuffing the fresh sea-air, and being comparatively free from the tyranny of my persecutor Sumunter, was truly indescribable." When they reach Aden, however, Burton demands that the abban be prosecuted. Surprisingly, Speke objects: "I was averse to punishing him, from the simple fact of having brought him over," a reason reflecting uneasiness with human conflict; a continuing, if perverse, attraction to his tormentor; a sense of guilt at not having lived up to expectations; and an instinctive opposition to Burton—if only because Sumunter had been his choice. "My commandant," says Speke, "thought otherwise, and that he had better be punished, if for no other reason than to set a good moral example to the others." The criticism is implicit though muted.[13]

But in at least two instances, not found in "Captain Speke's Adventures in Somali Land" but added in *What Led . . .* , Speke presses his grievance against Burton more directly. In the several years between publications, he had confirmed his claim to the Nile, and his falling out with Burton had greatly worsened. More sure of himself and also more angry, he attaches a note to Burton's claim of wanting to set a good moral example to others by prosecuting Sumunter: "this was a very dangerous policy to play with a people who consider might right, and revenge to death." This effectively lays the blame on Burton for the fight at

Berbera, with its disastrous consequences, that was soon to follow. The second point of dispute, concerning a suggestion of Burton's that the whole "system of Abbanship" should be done away with, is even sharper. Speke has sought an opinion, the substance of which he would have anticipated, from his friend and superior officer, Lieutenant-Colonel Robert Lambert Playfair, the Political Agent in Zanzibar, a long-standing opponent of Burton's, and another of the Indian Army bureaucrats whom Speke admired and Burton disliked. First, Speke protests that "this perhaps was scarcely the right time to dictate a policy which would be distasteful as well as injurious (in a monetary sense) to the people among whom we were about to travel, and with whom it was highly essential to be on the most friendly terms." Then, in a note, he gives Playfair's response as confirmation: " 'In this Lieutenant Burton erred; and this was the *termina causa* [sic] of all the mishaps which befell the expedition. The institution of Abbanage is of great antiquity, and is the representative amongst a barbarous people of our customs laws. . . .' "—or, we might say, our immigration laws, acceptance of an Abban representing assent to the force of local authority. Finally, and with considerable irony given Burton's dedication to native values and his skills in playing an Arab, Playfair makes the case for heeding local institutions: " 'A traveller who hopes for success in exploring a new country must accept the institutions he finds in existence. He can hardly hope, by his simple *fiat*, to revolutionise the time-honoured and *most profitable* institutions of a people, amongst whom precedent is a law as unchangeable as that of the Medes and the Persians.' " It is the voice of the boffin, albeit true enough. Playfair's opinion is exactly the one Speke was looking for: that Burton was the feckless architect of the disaster at Berbera.[14]

Berbera: The Caravan Leaves for Ogaden

Berbera lies south of Aden, some 200 miles across the Gulf. It became the capital of British Somaliland and today is said to have the longest runway, no doubt built by the Soviet Union, in all of Africa. A mid-twentieth-century atlas put its population at 20,000. In the nineteenth century it was the site of an annual fair, stretching from November to April, that brought vast numbers of traders with their caravans from all about the region. As many as 60,000 people may have swarmed into Berbera, where the Somalis traded slaves and cattle and ivory and rhinoceros horn for cloth, sheeting, metal goods, beads, dates, rice. Cruttenden described the scene in 1848: " 'During the height of the fair, Berbera is a perfect Babel, in confusion as in languages: no chief is acknowledged, and the customs of bygone days are the laws of the place. Disputes between the inland tribes daily arise, and are settled by the spear and dagger, the combatants retiring to the beach at a short distance from the town, in order that they may not disturb the trade.' " Anyone who has seen a modern African marketplace, even without Berbera's camels, donkeys, and conveyances, and without its warlike disputes, will have a faint idea of what Berbera was like in April 1855.[15]

For their venture into the interior, planned for the end of the fair, Burton had agreed with Outram that he would go in company with a caravan returning to the Ogaden region of (what is now) Ethiopia. Waiting for a ship to arrive in mid-April, Burton decided to let the caravan leave without him. This was his official explanation, though it is not completely certain what he expected the ship to deliver. In *First Footsteps*, he says he was awaiting "instruments and other necessaries by the mid-April mail from Europe." In an exculpatory report submitted to Brigadier William Coghlan, newly appointed Political Resident in Aden,[16] who was charged with investigating the Berbera disaster, he wrote that, "had our letters, sent from Aden, arrived within a moderate time, we should have been enabled to leave Berbera with the Ogadayn Caffilah." And he claims in *First Footsteps* that "the Ogadayn Caravan was anxious for our escort"—though it seems more likely that his superiors thought the Caravan should escort the expedition, rather than the other way around.[17]

Burton's biographers ordinarily, and probably correctly, take "instruments" to mean technical instruments, probably for surveying, sent (depending on which biography you read) "from Europe," "from London," or "from Bombay." Mary Lovell takes "letters" to mean "the mid-April mail from England, in which Richard undoubtedly hoped to hear news from his bereaved family"—his mother had died recently—"as well as reaction to his letter to Norton Shaw at the R.G.S"—that is, the Royal Geographical Society, of which Shaw, with whom Burton had been corresponding, was a prominent member and its Secretary. Maybe so, but would Burton have excused his imprudence to his superior officer because he was awaiting personal "letters"? "Letters" and "instruments" might even be roughly the same thing, official documents intended to smooth the path of the expedition on its way. Lovell gives no source for saying that surveying instruments had been ordered from Bombay or that Burton "undoubtedly" hoped to hear from his family. Of course no biographer can footnote every detail, and every biographer has to improvise sometimes, but uncertainty remains. Perhaps Burton *wanted* Coghlan to think he was waiting for official documents while really waiting for mail and surveying instruments. Like Isabel, Lovell thinks Burton warm-hearted, likely to be waiting for mail and for comfort from home—but also prudent: she believes he would have been "only too happy to join forces" with the Ogaden caravan.[18]

Yet Burton also gives a glimpse, in *First Footsteps*, of another less prudential, more Burtonian reason for his unhappy decision, a reason that precedes the "official" one: "we wished to witness the close of the Berberah fair," and—secondarily—"we expected instruments and other necessaries by the mid-April mail from Europe." It would have been like Burton, ever the proto-anthropologist, to want to see the fair to its end—and also like him to find reasons for going it on his own rather than submitting to the chaperonage of the Ogaden caravan. I think we cannot know that he would have been happy to join the caravan if only the mail had arrived in time.[19]

Speke's version of what happened at this critical moment, rather lumbering and far less crisp than Burton's, increases the odds that the ship from Aden was to have brought surveying instruments, for Speke calls the missing letters and instruments, tangible "things": "At this time we were daily expecting a vessel from Aden, which would bring us some letters and instruments that were on their way out from England, and saw the great Ugahden caravan preparing to leave, but were undecided what to do—whether to go with them without our things from England, or wait and rely upon our strength in travelling alone. The latter alternative was unfortunately decided upon . . ." If Speke was less authoritative as a writer than Burton, he was also, here, more circumspect. Burton's account is not inflected by any sense of deliberation. What happened, happened. Speke, on the contrary, indicates that alternatives were weighed: "the latter alternative was unfortunately decided upon." Of course he needed, at first writing, to be careful before accusing his superior officer directly of imprudence. But if the decision was made communally, as the passive voice suggests, he would seem to be admitting some responsibility for the consequences that followed. It was a tricky rhetorical impasse that he tried to alleviate by adding, in *What Led* . . . , certain inconspicuous asides that directly incriminated his superior.[20]

Berbera: The Attack

What followed, now, was a military and human disaster; and, for Burton and Speke, a keystone of all their troubles.

According to Burton (in "Captain Speke"), Speke misrepresented what happened during the attack, by a band of angry Somalis, at one or two in the morning of April 19, 1855: "he gives the world to understand that he alone of the force had attempted to defend the camp." This exaggerates, but not outrageously, Speke's self-described role. In *What Led* . . . , Speke says he had given "strict orders" not to waste ammunition "in firing to frighten, or giving false alarms." When he heard musket fire, aimed over the heads of three visitors who arrived just after sundown on April 18—spies, they turned out to be—"my anger knew no bounds. All hopes of security seemed annihilated by such direct disobedience to all order." The responsibility for order and for giving orders, on this account, shifts into Speke's own hands. What the men should have done, presuming the visitors were hostile, would have been to "fire into, and not over, their object."[21]

Had any such orders been followed, things might have turned out differently. Worse still, Burton misread the visitors' intentions, concluding "that their coming . . . was accidental, and not designed," another instance when his acumen fails. The great adventurer is gullible, the victim of "Eastern" people, who "from constant practice . . . forge lies with far greater facility" than truth. Of the charges against him, this one, attacking both his power of command and his pride in knowing native peoples, must have galled Burton badly, especially if it was true. Hiring Sumunter and Ahmed and failing to leave Berbera with the Ogaden caravan are venial mistakes compared to ignoring a threat to the safety of his men.[22]

When the attack occurs, Speke reports that "I bounced out of bed, with pistol and dirk in hand, and ran across to the central tent to know what was the matter, and if we were to have any shooting." While Speke "bounces" into action, runs eagerly to the central tent, and is ready for the fray, Burton is clumsily "occupied in trying to load his revolver." The game hunter from the Himalayas is more adept and better prepared for a fight than his commander. Burton, on this account, is slow to load and maybe slow on the draw. The insinuation that he didn't know how to handle a gun cannot have pleased him any more than the insinuation that he didn't understand indigenous peoples.[23]

It is remarkable that Burton and Speke both survived the attack, as Lieutenant William Stroyan did not, though each was severely wounded and Speke narrowly came away with his life. During the combat, his revolver jammed and he was overpowered by his attackers. Lying on the ground, he feared he was about to be castrated or killed, but the men spoke to him in Arabic and he replied "in broken Somali"—if so, Speke had somewhat more linguistic ability than Burton gave him credit for[24]—"and heard them say they had not killed any of the English, and would not kill me." Why they would not have killed Speke, since Stroyan had in fact been killed brutally, is uncertain; but eventually Speke managed to escape, suffering many wounds, eluding "at least forty . . . men," and, as Burton wrote quite admiringly in *First Footsteps*, running "the gauntlet of a score of missiles." The escape "was in every way wonderful." Nor did Burton ever retract what amounted to oblique praise. In "Captain Speke:" "Speke escaped as by a miracle." Burton himself suffered a spear wound through his cheek, leaving the scar that ever after enhanced his appearance of diabolical intensity.[25]

It was at the very onset of the attack that Burton offended Speke most deeply. We may think the offense a small thing, but it was not one for a soldier, especially not a soldier like Speke, to take lightly. As the fighting started, he says, "I . . . ran under lee of the fly of the tent to take a better survey, and, by stooping low, could perceive the heads of some men peeping like monkeys over the boxes. Lieutenant Burton now said, 'Don't step back, or they will think we are retiring.' Chagrined by this rebuke at my management in fighting, and imagining by the remark I was expected to defend the camp, I stepped boldly to the front, and fired at close quarters into the first man before me." As Burton tells it, "I unwittingly offended Lieut. Speke's susceptibilities by saying in the thick of the fight, 'Don't step back, or they'll think we are running.'" The context of the admonition varies considerably in its two versions. According to Speke, he had already sheltered himself under the fly of the tent, the better to estimate the strength and position of the enemy. According to Burton, the offending words came "in the thick of the fight," implying that Speke had welcomed a chance to escape the line of fire. In Speke's version, Burton must have known that he was not "retiring" or "running." In fact Speke's version is questionable: Burton would hardly have told him not to step back if he had already taken a fixed position under the tent and already spotted the heads of men (in his gratuitous analogy) "peeping like monkeys" over the boxes. And Speke's statement that he imagined he "was expected to defend the camp" is curious: what else was he supposed to be doing? All in all, Burton gets somewhat the better of the story. But of course he had the advantage, having found out that he had given offense: "as usual I was never allowed to know that he was 'chagrined by this rebuke at his management' till his own account of the mishap appeared before the public." The story of Burton and Speke is particularly sad at this point: two brave men falling out over an admonition, at a very dangerous moment, that can only have been instinctive and not ill intended.[26]

Disputing what he sees as Speke's effort to take all the credit for defending the camp, Burton portrays him now as having lost control: "The fact is, he had lost his head, and instead of following me when cutting my way through the enemy, he rushed about, dealing blows with the butt of an unloaded revolver." If Speke had only followed me, it is Burton's claim, he would have escaped more easily, for Burton was an exceptional swordsman. In Speke's account, we hear nothing of blows with the butt of the revolver that Burton says was "unloaded," but, instead, of several shots at the enemy. About these events in Berbera, which brought the incipient expedition to its untimely end and cast a dark shadow over all that followed, there was nothing on which the two men could afford to agree.[27]

"Lieutenant Speke's Diary"

In "Captain Speke," Burton dismisses the journal that Speke kept during his unhappy search for the Wadi Nogal as deficient in every respect: "He had recorded his misadventures in a diary whose style, to say nothing of sentiments and geographical assertions, rendered it, in my opinion, unfit for publication." Since the original journal does not survive, we can know it only by inferring the use Speke later made of it, with whatever amendments. There is no doubt, however, that Burton did what he claims to have done with the original manuscript Speke had handed over to him: "I took the trouble of re-writing the whole." It was during their subsequent expedition to the lakes that Burton learned of the offence he had given: "Some two years afterwards, when in the heart of Africa, and half delirious with fever, my companion let fall certain expressions which, to my infinite surprise, showed that he had been nursing three great grievances. The front of the offence was that his Diary had been spoiled . . ." The other grievances were that Speke had "derived no profit" from his own story; and that Burton had sent his collection of wildlife specimens to the Calcutta Museum of Natural History.[28]

Speke might not have taken offence at Burton's rewrite had he not been inspired to do so by his friend Laurence Oliphant—novelist, diplomat, travel writer, satirist, a homosexual who took pride in his sexless marriage, a "mystic in lavender kid gloves," a troublemaker, and all in all, a strange Victorian case.[29] It was Oliphant who reviewed *First Footsteps* in *Blackwood's*, expressing regret that "the experiences of one whose extensive wanderings had already so well qualified him for the task, and who has shown himself so able an explorer, should not have been chronicled at greater length, and thrown into a form which would have rendered them more interesting to the general reader." This comment, Burton is convinced, "kindled a fire which did not consume the less fiercely because it was smothered." Mary Lovell concurs: Oliphant persuaded Speke that Burton "not only plagiarised his work, but had deliberately damaged" it. Yet, to stick with Burton's metaphor, where there is fire, the fire danger is likely to have been high. Less clever than Burton, Speke was hardly insensitive to games of power. Oliphant's remark, in a long review that otherwise praised *First Footsteps* highly, may have been the spark. But whether the review fostered Speke's resentment matters less in the long run than the question, did he have serious reason to take offence?[30]

Lovell thinks not, believing Speke bordered on the irrational: "A more rational man might have realised that there was an obvious solution." Though Speke's behavior over time did become increasingly strange, the "obvious solution" in this case is not entirely obvious: "Richard had used only 40 pages (it comprised less than 10 per cent of *First Footsteps*), so there was no reason why"—had it indeed been publishable—"Speke should not still publish." Maybe, yes; more likely, no. Any sensible publisher would have had doubts about putting in print what would have been in some measure used goods, even granting that Burton had printed "only" 40 pages. And Speke's unpolished style would not have been likely to attract a publisher or appeal much to public taste before he had laid claim to the Nile, no matter that he had travelled alone and explored new territory. With his claim to the Nile, however, the journal became eminently publishable, and Speke had grounds, at least in retrospect, for resenting Burton's takeover. At the same time, though he may have been unhappy about it, he accepted Burton's superior rank and precedence. In a footnote that he attached to the text of *What Led . . .* , he says, with apparent acquiescence: "These notes were reported in an Appendix in the 'First Footsteps in East Africa,' by Lieutenant Burton, with his other reports of the expedition." In a court of law—not that it would ever have come to that—Burton would have been found quite innocent of any wrong doing.[31]

More than any question of publishability, however, Speke could reasonably have resented the preemption of his identity. The journal, as Burton printed it, is in the third person, a chronicle of the "Diary and Observations made by Lieutenant Speke, When Attempting to Reach the Wady Nogal," with interpolations by Burton himself: "it was in the third person, without the least intention of giving offense, but simply because I did not wish to palm off upon the reader my own composition as that of another person." The tension lies between divergent attributions of authorship. What Burton gives the reader is something different from "Speke's" diary. Sometimes it is of Burton's "own composition." One interpolation criticizes Speke as a geographer: "After descending about 2,000 feet from the crest of the mountains to the southern fall, Lieutenant Speke entered upon the platform which forms the country of the Eastern Somal. He is persuaded that the watershed of this extensive tract is from N.W. to S.E., contrary to the opinion of Lieutenant Cruttenden, who, from information derived from the Somal, determined the slope to be due south." Speke is wrong, Burton implies; Cruttenden, right. And, in another interpolation near the end, Burton lets it be known that Sumunter "is now by the just orders of the acting Political Resident, Aden, expiating his divers offences in the Station Jail"—"just orders" responding to Burton's decision, contrary to Speke's wish, that the abban should be arraigned at the bar of British justice. "Lieutenant Speke's Diary" is as much or more a story of how Burton was the presiding intelligence behind these "first footsteps" in East Africa (though they were not that, really, German missionaries and others having been there already). Burton even affixes his own last word to the "Diary," an apostrophe to the virtues and values of British colonialism: "Lastly, we cannot expect great things without some establishment at Berberah." A British agent, if there were one, could license abbans to protect strangers, and "nothing would tend more surely than this measure to open up the new country to commerce and civilization."[32]

By putting Burton's redaction against Speke's later, published accounts, we can cautiously infer something of what Burton does to the original; and then, in turn, as cautiously infer something of Speke's own revisions. His entries for the month of December 1855 in *What Led . . .* run to perhaps 7500 words; Burton's edit, to perhaps 4000. Of the 3500 words "missing" in the edit, some no doubt are from Speke's letters to his mother and were not included in the original journal. Any conclusions about Burton's editing job or about Speke's revisions of his original, whether in response to Burton's edit or otherwise, must be taken as speculations.

Among the changes Speke seems to have made, he deletes any reference to the axis of the watershed in "the eastern Somal" that, Burton thought, ran not northwest-southeast but due south. Probably Speke is conceding the point. Another discrepancy that points to revision concerns the Yafir pass. In "Lieutenant Speke's Diary," the altitude is given as "about 7,500 feet." Speke himself puts it instead at precisely 6704 feet. We cannot know for sure whether he is correcting himself or, instead, Burton's use of his notes. But since he could have had no new empirical evidence, the chances are he is correcting Burton. If so, he wants us to know that he is not so imprecise a geographer as to have given the height of the pass as "about 7,500 feet."[33] In effect he is saying: see how unreliable my companion is, he can't even get plain facts right.[34]

In comparing the entries for December 4, 1854, from "Lieutenant Speke's Diary" and from Speke himself, certain of Burton's editing habits emerge, as do differences of attitude and character that divide the travellers. The entries, describing Speke's ascent of the Yafir Pass, show him as the truer romantic of the two; the romantic Burton, more tough-minded and matter-of-fact, for he recasts the soft stone of Speke's original in a much harder mold.

Speke: *4th December 1854*.—" . . . [T]he face of the mountain-top, towering to a great height, stood frowning over us like a huge bluff wall, which at first sight it appeared quite impossible any camel could surmount. At 9 A. M. we reached this steep, and commenced the stiffest and last ascent up a winding, narrow goat-path, having sharp turns at the extremity of every zigzag, and with huge projecting stones, which seemed to bid defiance to the passage of the camels' bodies. Indeed, it was very marvellous, with their long spindle-shanks and great splay feet, and the awkward boxes on their backs striking constantly against every little projection in the hill, that they did not tumble headlong over the pathway . . . . The ascent was at length completed after an infinity of trouble, and our view from the top of the mountain repaid me fully for everything of the past. It was a glorious place! In one glance round I had a complete survey of all the country I was now destined to travel over, and what I had already gone over."[35]

This could be Wordsworth, though in rather stolid prose: the "towering" mountain and its great stone face recall a famous mountain of Wordsworth's childhood in *The Prelude*. Everywhere Speke evokes the natural sublime. The mountain towers and frowns like a huge wall, it seems impossible to surmount, its projecting stones are huge, the camels' ability to climb it is marvelous, the ascent requires an infinity of trouble, the view from the top is—though Speke does not say so—sublime, the panorama takes in the horizon on either side: "It was a glorious place!"—one among the many heights climbed by romantic poets and travellers, inspiring intimations of the infinite such as Speke hints at obliquely in his "infinity of trouble."

What does Burton do with these mountainous feelings? "About dawn the caravan was loaded, and then proceeded along a tolerably level pathway through a thick growth of thorn trees towards a bluff hill. The steep was reached about 9 A.M., and the camels toiled up the ascent by a stony way, dropping their loads for want of ropes, and stumbling on their road. The summit, about 500 yards distant, was reached in an hour. At Yafir, on the crest of the mountains, the caravan halted two hours for refreshment. Lieutenant Speke describes the spot in the enthusiastic language of all travellers who have visited the Seaward Range of the Somali Hills." Gone is any hint of the sublime, replaced by measured estimate: the pathway is tolerably level, the camels can't help stumbling, the summit is (a mere) 500 yards from the starting point, reaching it takes an hour. Enthusiasm and enthusiastic language are hallmarks of an amateur. Like other travellers, Speke revels in amateur emotions. As for "all" the travellers to the Somali Hills, how many had there been? In the phrase of a British friend who read this book while it was in manuscript, Burton here and elsewhere is over-egging the pudding.[36]

Sometimes Burton's editing seems finicky at best. In entries for December 8 and 9, soon after the ascent of the Yafir pass, Speke writes in *What Led* . . . : "The distance accomplished was eight miles when we put up in the Kraal of Rhut . . . Rhut is the most favoured spot in the Warsingali dominions." Then: "Halt. Kin's City. Or rather the ruins of it, I was told, lay to the northward of my camp . . ." All this appears in "Lieutenant Speke's Diary," as: "On the 9th of December Lieutenant Speke, halting at Rhat, visited one of 'Kin's' cities, now ruined by time, and changed by the Somal having converted it into a cemetery."[37]

It is another case when no one would worry about the details, were it not for the larger environment of combat. Speke's "Kraal of Rhut" is Burton's "Rhat." Speke's "Kin's City" is "one of 'Kin's' cities." Burton was almost obsessional in his concern for orthography, as is evident from the marginal comments he made in his books. These could be cases of Speke correcting Burton's transcription but are far more likely cases of Burton amending Speke. His re-rendering of "Kin's City. Or rather the ruins of it" as "one of Kin's cities, now ruined by time" is the smallest of matters yet symptomatic: Burton knows he is not only a much better linguist but a more euphonious writer. In his copy of Stanley's *Through the Dark Continent* (1878), finding the words "I dressed myself and sauntered . . . ," he draws a line through "myself," no doubt on grounds that "myself" is redundant. Tinkering with Speke's prose, as with Stanley's, he asserts more than just rhetorical superiority.[38]

Burton may also appropriate some material from Speke that cannot then be easily recycled. On the archaeology of "Kin's City," Speke gives only physical descriptions, e.g., "The plan of the church is an oblong square, 48 by 27 feet, its length lying N.E. and S.W., whilst its breadth was directed N.W. and S.E., which latter may be considered its front and rear." Burton gives diagrams and illustrations. Either they are taken from Speke or are Burton's own reconstructions. But even Burton would have been hard put to devise illustrations on the basis of nothing more than physical description. Most likely, the illustrations come from Speke. If so, he probably felt his work had been confiscated.[39]

On occasion Speke had reason, even if he did not realize it, to be grateful to his editor. In an entry for December 10, Burton seems to save him embarrassment by passing over the day's events with a brief, though tantalizing notice: "Before quitting Rhat, the Abban and the interpreter went to the length of ordering Lieutenant Speke not to fire a gun. This detained him a whole day." What can possibly have happened?[40]

Speke tells us. And, as in the trial of Sumunter, he comes across as laughable, almost a caricature of the British colonial, and inept, an inadequate leader: "I rose early and ordered the men to load, but not a soul would stir. The Abban had ordered otherwise, and they all preferred to stick, like brother villains, to him. And then began a battle-royal; as obstinately as I insisted, so obstinately did he persist; then, to show his superior authority, and thinking to touch me on a tender point, forbade my shooting any more." The roles of the leader and the guide, always in some tension, are subject here to intense strain. For the eager sportsman, the outrage is not to be borne: "This was too much for my now heated blood to stand, so I immediately killed a partridge running on the ground before his face." It is irresistibly funny (except, no doubt, to the poor and blameless victim) to imagine Speke blasting away at a partridge on the ground, against all the conventions of sport, to show Sumunter who is in charge. When Sumunter then says he will kill Speke if he dares shoot again, things get nastier. Cooler heads prevail, however, and after negotiations, the dust-up comes to an end. It is silly, if dangerous, and Speke manages a dry epilogue: "Thus ended this valuable day." Perhaps he knew he had cut a foolish figure.[41]

Finally, is there any telling what Burton found objectionable in Speke's "sentiments"? It would be more agreeable to overlook the question because the probable answer requires lingering over British-Indian attitudes and a distressing epithet that was common coin of the imperial realm. In the rare nineteen-page pamphlet, *My Second Expedition to Eastern Intertropical Africa* (1860), published in Cape Town while Speke was on his way with Grant to confirm his claim to the Nile—a text later reprinted, not quite entire, in *What Led . . .*—he describes a group of porters in Mombasa: "Noise and dancing seemed their principal delight, and they indulged in it, blowing horns and firing muskets with a boisterous glee. . . . They were jolly niggers." In *What Led . . .* , the porters' noise and dancing and boisterous glee are all still there; but "jolly niggers" are gone. By 1864, Speke—or his publishers—realized the problem. Similarly, an allusion to his servant Bombay, lovingly intended, as looking like a "tobacconist's jolly nigger" in the "Journal of a Cruise on the Tanzania Lake" is made marginally more proper in *What Led . . .* by inverted commas around " 'jolly nigger' "—ensuring that we do not forget the allusion is (only) to a trade sign.[42]

" 'Jack was an Anglo-Indian,' " says Burton, according to Isabel in her biography, " 'without any knowledge of Eastern manners and customs and religion, and of any Oriental language beyond broken Hindostanee.' " And " 'Anglo-Indians, as everybody knows, often take offence without reason' "—most likely including the offence Speke had taken at Burton's appropriation of his journal; " 'they expect civility as their *due*, they treat all skins a shade darker than their own' "—we remember that Burton was very dark—" 'as "niggers," and Arabs are, or can be, the most courteous gentlemen, and exceedingly punctilious.' " To which Isabel adds a note: "The Arabs always gave Richard the most courteous and cordial reception, treating him practically as one of themselves. They could not be expected to think so much of Speke, because he did not know their language or their religion, and he always treated them as an Anglo-Indian treats a nigger." Did Speke, in a moment of impatience or illness or ill-chosen jest, call Burton, with his darker skin, a nigger to his face?[43]

Anglo-Indian attitudes probably account for many of Speke's "sentiments" that Burton disliked, including a view of Africans as simpleminded negroes, the description of the attackers at Berbera as peeping over boxes like monkeys, and the image of Sumunter and his family as badgers in their hut. To these might be added a Grand Guignol narrative, omitted in "Captain Speke's Adventures in Somali Land" but prominent in *What Led* . . . , of a scuffle between an African woman and Speke's interpreter. The interpreter seizes one of Speke's revolvers and chases her playfully, the woman then "bounced on a bench and poked her tail in my man's face," and the interpreter, unaware the gun is loaded, fires two bullets "into her fleshy projection." Speke is pressed into service as a surgeon for want of anyone more qualified, though the woman is "bashful": "It was certainly very amusing to witness the struggle between virtue and necessity, and the operation was so far satisfactory that I succeeded in extracting one of the balls." If this "odd accident" was in the journal that Burton edited (as perhaps it was not), he is not likely to have found it very amusing.[44]

In India Burton's fellow officers had called him the "White Nigger," sometimes amiably, sometimes not, and he himself referred to natives whom he liked as "niggers" to mark his solidarity with them. The epithet was in common usage, up and down the ranks of Anglo-India. Burton's dislike for things Anglo-Indian, including the derogatory language of imperial power, arose from experience. No doubt he thought he was doing Speke a favor by cleaning up the journal—as in some respects he was. Not that Burton himself harbored any doubt that Africans were an inferior race, but he would not have thought the epithet befitting, coming from such a stereotypical Anglo-Indian as John Hanning Speke.[45]

Yet Speke could not have been expected to welcome the favor Burton had done him, even if he did come to realize, or to accept the opinion of his publishers, that "jolly niggers" would have been a blemish on his narrative. I think he would not have been assuaged to learn that Burton did not profit from *First Footsteps*. I also think the dispatch of his specimens to Calcutta was of no major importance. What counted most, even if Speke could not have articulated his feelings well: the submergence of his self-identity within the larger-than-life image of the darkly devilish Richard Burton.

CHAPTER FIVE

Seeking the Nile

Burton published *First Footsteps*, with its redaction of Speke's journal, in 1856 and, late in the same year, the two of them went off together again to seek the Nile. It was a partnership of convenience, for Speke was already furious at his companion, whom he called "a rotter" in a letter to his mother. Setting off from London on their way to Bombay and then to Zanzibar, the travellers must have eyed each other warily, Speke harboring suppressed resentment, Burton unaware how much offense Speke had taken but very likely sensing that he was not wholly at ease. For his part, Speke would have felt that, as he had suffered with Sumunter, he was now about to suffer again with another difficult companion who happened to be his superior and without whom he would never achieve his goal. In Mary Lovell's account, Speke "still stood in semi-awe of Burton, and in Burton's ability to get things done"; but "semi-awe" goes oddly together with suppressed resentment. Burton, Lovell thinks, "saw only the quiet charm of his tall, fair companion." "Why else," she asks, "should he invite him to join the most important project he had ever undertaken?" An answer might be: because in the charm of this tall, fair companion, and in the darkness of Burton's own countenance, lay the seeds of mutual attraction—it need not have been homosexual, if certainly homoerotic—that bound these mighty opposites together and shaped their ends.[1] Lovell, again: "far more complex than Richard's decision to take Speke were Speke's motives in joining Richard." But has anyone ever thought that Burton was an uncomplicated man?[2]

What bound the two immediately together, against all rational sense, was the Nile. To find its mysterious source would mean immediate fame and probable fortune for having solved a geographical puzzle more than 2,000 years old. Nor was it only because the puzzle was venerable, or because of its promised rewards, that it so engaged the imagination. Reaching the source of the great and fertile Nile, the river of Osiris, would be like finding the beginnings of life itself and its systolic rhythms: "you are the Nile," runs a hymn to Osiris, "gods and men live from your overflow." Humankind is always on the hunt for the *fons et origo* of things. In the same year as Burton and Speke returned to England after their journey, there appeared *On the Origin of Species by Means of Natural Selection.*

The allure of the source is pervasive, extending to small moments of experience as well as to the grandeur of the Nile or the mystery of speciation. Most summers I go horseback riding in the Sierra Nevada, sometimes riding upwards from a valley floor at six thousand feet to high lakes at nine thousand feet. After a steep climb through trees, there is a fine panorama. The wrangler leading the ride will stop and point down to a dark green patch on the valley floor: "That is the source of the West Walker." It does not matter that the West branch of the Walker River is a small tributary in the large ecosystem of the eastern Sierra. The glimpse from such a vantage of a river at its point of origin calls up the feelings, quite primordial, that the beginnings of any river, the Mississippi or the Amazon or the Walker, inspire. And the Nile is the river of all rivers, not only the longest but the most lavish in its gifts. Who would not have yearned to find its source?

And when Speke, having left Burton behind in Kazeh, finally gazed out at what is now called Lake Victoria, how did he know he had reached his goal? On the face of it he had no evidence, but the heart has its reasons, and it was an intuitive leap—to Burton's scorn—that led Speke to stake his claim. The flow of the Nile, he would have realized, ran due north of Lake Victoria, and the direct longitudinal line amounts to the hint of a reason; Lake Tanganyika, from which Burton and also David Livingstone believed that the Nile flowed, lies to the west, though in early maps barely to the west, of the northern lake. The roughly uterine shape of Lake Victoria, of which an Arab informant, Snay bin Amir, had given the travellers a fair sense[3]—and which an observer at the south shore may intuit—probably also played a part in his inspired guess. Christopher Ondaatje, following Speke on his journeys and standing on the south shore of the lake, describes the feeling: "It is a phenomenal sight. Its vastness . . . is stunning. . . . Even though I was far better prepared for the sight than Speke could have been, I was, like Speke, overcome by it. It was no longer a surprise to me that Speke could make that tremendous leap of faith. Faced by its majesty, anyone would accept that this was a lake of vital geographical importance." I have stood there myself—and, at very least, nothing seems outlandish in Speke's leap of faith, even granting that we know what he could only guess at. Did Burton realize from the start that his impulsive companion's intuition might be right? Two less considerable egos might have agreed to collaborate once again and try to confirm the truth or establish the untruth of Speke's belief, but that was not to be.[4]

Burton v. Speke: *The Lake Regions*

With his usual industry, Burton published the two large volumes of *The Lake Regions of Central Africa: A Picture of Exploration* in early 1860, only a year after he returned. He had hoped to publish even sooner and was unhappy that the delay had allowed Speke to beat him into print in *Blackwood's*: "I had intended this record of personal adventure to appear immediately after my return to Europe, in May 1859. The impaired health, the depression of spirits, and worse still the annoyance of official correspondence,"—much of it about events at Berbera—"which to me have been the sole results of African Exploration, may be admitted as valid reasons for the delay." After this testy prelude, Burton goes on to revenge himself on Speke, not only for having beaten him into print but above all for having robbed him of his prerogative: a quasi-imperial right to the territory of the lakes and, thus, to the source of the Nile, wherever it might lie. More than Speke's temerity or the violation of a promise in going to the Royal Geographical Society first, the impetuous decision by the president of the Society, Sir Roderick Murchison, that Speke should be the standard bearer for the next expedition infuriated Burton. Rich, distinguished, and powerful, Murchison was a gentleman geologist whom a biographer calls a "scientist of empire"—exactly the sort of authority figure Burton had trouble getting along with. If Murchison had not accepted Speke's view, and if he had not said (in Speke's account), " 'Speke, we must send you there again,' " thus cutting Burton out, Burton's grievance would have been far less great. His anger is partly displaced anger at the Society and at Murchison; Speke is the less risky, more vulnerable target. In *The Lake Regions*, Burton does all he can to damage the standing of his antagonist—even as Speke and Grant were preparing, and then embarking on, their new expedition. If he could discredit Speke, Burton would be vindicated and the authority of the Society also discredited. The fact that the Society had awarded Burton its gold medal only days after he returned in May 1859 was no consolation, nor was Murchison's effort to seem publicly impartial.[5] Burton had lost the game.[6]

The combat breaks into view in the preface to *The Lake Regions*: "I have spoken out my feelings concerning Captain Speke, my companion in the Expedition which forms the subject of these pages. The history of our companionship is simply this . . ." It is as "my companion" that Speke appears throughout the pages of *The Lake Regions*, a companion- ship gilded with irony and even scorn. Samuel Johnson, in his *Dictio-*

nary, gives a subsidiary meaning of "companion," of which Burton would have been aware: "a familiar term of contempt." Johnson's examples come from Shakespeare's *Henry IV*, Part 2: "I scorn you, scurvy companion;" and from Raleigh: "It gives boldness to every petty companion to spread rumours to my defamation, in places where I cannot be present." The one from Raleigh is almost eerily pertinent. Only in the preface and once at the very end does Burton's companion appear as "Captain Speke."[7]

Now Burton opens direct fire: "The history of our companionship is simply this:—As he had suffered with me in purse and person at Berberah in 1855, I thought it but just to offer him the opportunity of renewing an attempt to penetrate into Africa. I had no other reasons." That is, Speke had nothing of substance to contribute to the expedition. "I could not expect much from his assistance; he was not a linguist— French and Arabic being equally unknown to him—nor a man of science, nor an accurate astronomical observer." It was Burton who obtained leave for Speke after it had been officially refused, and "during the exploration he acted in a subordinate capacity; . . . he was unfit for any other but a subordinate capacity." This is very pointed, given that Speke by then had been assigned by the Society to lead the expedition that would confirm his findings. So: "Can I then feel otherwise than indignant, when I find that, after preceding me from Aden to England, with the spontaneous offer, on his part, of not appearing before the Society that originated the Expedition until my return, he had lost no time in taking measures to secure for himself the right of working the field which I had opened . . . ?" The debate about the Nile subsides in importance next to the undermining of what Burton thought was his by right, the field that he "had opened." Nor, he says, was the Nile even the real object of his quest. Rather, he had applied to the Society to ascertain the limits of the "Sea of Ujiji"—Lake Tanganyika—and "to determine the exportable produce of the interior, and the ethnography of its tribes." The quest for the Nile is just a craze, the grapes are sour: "In these days every explorer of Central Africa is supposed to have set out in quest of the coy sources of the White Nile, and when he returns without them, his exploration, whatever may have been its value, is determined to be a failure." The Nile is a vulgar passion. The real issue, and in a sense it *was* the real issue: the riches of Africa were objects of an explorers' land rush. Burton believes Speke has stolen his valuable property.[8]

In *The Lake Regions*, Burton abridges Speke's part in the story, portraying him as weak, weakly, even unsound of mind; and, in the matter of the Nile, impressionable and girlish in his leap of faith. Even granting Burton his reasons, it is fierce revenge. "My companion" is a faint presence, emerging from Burton's shadow only in sickness or in unflattering glimpses. Small wonder that, when they met at Bath on the day before their planned debate in 1864, Speke rushed off, unable to speak to Burton or to share the platform with his intractable opponent for more than a passing moment.

The expedition to the lakes was ravaged, again and again, by illness. Burton was not immune. For example: "I arose weak and depressed, with aching head, burning eyes, and throbbing extremities." Or: "I again suffered from fever; the attack, after lasting seven days, disappeared, leaving, however, hepatic complications." And: "I lay for a fortnight upon the earth, too blind to read or write, except with long intervals, too weak to ride, and too ill to converse." Whatever Burton's own ailments, however, Speke's are displayed more prominently. Almost every time we see him, he is ill. These are index entries, by far the majority of those under Speke's name: "his illness in Uzaramo"; "shakes off his preliminary symptoms"; "lays the foundations of a fever"; "thoroughly prostrated"; "recovers his health"; "again attacked"; "and by 'liver' at Rumuma"; "dangerous illness'; "restored"; "unable to walk"; "tormented by ophthalmia"; "a beetle in his ear"; "improvement in his health"; and, finally, "his deafness and dimness of vision"—this last entry preceding, ironically and immediately, "leaves Kazeh for the North," Speke's solo journey to the Victoria Nyanza. Burton, too, was ill at the time: "I suffered severely from swelling and numbness of the extremities." But Speke's ailment prevents him "from reading, writing, and"—crucially—"observing correctly." Though Speke recovers health before leaving for the lake, Burton would not mind if we supposed his companion's ability to observe correctly had been permanently damaged.[9]

And, in one crucial, early episode in *The Lake Regions*, Burton interprets an illness of Speke's as having resulted in mental impairment. The travellers are crossing the Rubeho pass, called the Pass Terrible, in an ascent to 5700 feet, a crossing that inspires Burton to prose as florid as Speke's in his panorama from the Yafir Pass, but with a difference. Where Speke tapped the sunny Wordsworthian vein, Burton's panorama is Gothic—rocks and boulders emerge from "a shaggy growth of mountain vegetation"; "forest glens and hanging woods" are "black with shade"—and more painterly: "A glowing sun gilded the canopy of dense smoke which curtained the nearer plain, and in the background the hazy atmosphere painted with azure the broken wall of hill . . . ." Notwithstanding the surgery he had performed on Speke's high style, Burton had nothing against the high style when it was his own. And here, in the Pass Terrible (with its suggestion of Bunyanesque allegory), Speke falls seriously ill. "I was compelled to halt," Burton says. "My invalid sub. had been seized with a fever-fit that induced a dangerous delirium during two successive nights; he became so violent that it was necessary to remove his weapons, and, to judge from certain symptoms, the attack had a permanent cerebral effect. Death appeared stamped upon his features . . . ." The Pass Terrible lives up to its name.[10]

"My invalid sub." is very condescending: not only is Speke sick and delirious but, as it were permanently, an invalid and forever a subaltern, unfit to lead. Yet the portrayal of his delirium has both the ring of truth and more than a hint of the terrible, here in the mountain pass so well named. What violence did Speke threaten that required his weapons to be taken away: murder or suicide? Both? In his delirium, might he have acted out the desire to come to Africa and be killed? Did his hatred of

Burton fan homicidal fantasies? The Pass Terrible is a site of Conradian darkness; Speke's face, an image of death, stamped like a mask on his features. And he will suffer, in the aftermath, "certain symptoms" that indicate "a permanent cerebral effect."

What were the "symptoms" underlying this verdict—it is nothing less—of madness? It would not have been at all crazy for Speke to preempt Burton's claim to central Africa by beating him to the Royal Geographical Society. That would have been rational self-interest—even if, in the calculus of proper conduct between officers and gentlemen, it would have been dubious behavior. Otherwise, Burton refers to symptoms that cannot be surely identified but may include accusations by Speke that Burton tried unsuccessfully to induce "Bombay," Speke's devoted friend and guide, to poison him as they were returning to the coast. And, while on their return, Speke suffered another, still more serious episode of delirium, during which he blurted out his grievances against Burton. Mary Lovell reports a similar case, also in East Africa, of feverish mania and paranoia that ended in the victim's suicide. "Did something like this," she wonders, "permanently affect Speke, as Richard suspected? Probably we shall never know . . ." I would say, we will certainly never know. "Certain symptoms" and "permanent cerebral effect" are tantalizing. Either Burton is giving a non-specific account of recurrent mania; or he is building his case against his companion by simply calling him insane.[11]

Yet Speke is not only deranged in Burton's story, he is also comic, once more a knight of doleful countenance. In March 1858, Burton had dispatched his companion on a mission from Ujiji, on the eastern shore of Lake Tanganyika. His assignment was to hire a dhow to explore the northern reaches of the lake—and to locate the hoped-for outlet of the Nile. The mission, like that in search of the Wadi Nogal, failed miserably. Speke returned after a month with no dhow and little to show for his efforts except some shells, previously unknown, from the western shore and a new measurement of the width of the lake. Unhappy with the outcome, Burton stages a dramatic comedy: "On the 29th of March the rattling of matchlocks announced my companion's return"—noises, as it were, off. Then Speke appears from the wings, soaked by seasonal rains: "The Masika"—the rains—"had done its worst upon him. I never saw a man so thoroughly moist and mildewed; he justified even the French phrase 'wet to the bone.' His paraphernalia were in a similar state; his guns were grained with rust, and his fire-proof powder-magazine had admitted the monsoon-rain." Damp and bedraggled, moist and mildewed, Speke has not even managed to keep his powder dry.[12]

On the journey, he had also suffered extremely when a beetle invaded his ear and, despite going after it with a pen-knife, he could not dislodge it. The resulting infection, in Speke's words, was "the most painful thing I ever remember to have endured." Burton relegates this episode in *The Lake Regions* to a long footnote, reproducing Speke's account of it from *Blackwood's*, while in the main text, Speke's damp condition and his ear infection are conjoined: "When my companion had somewhat recovered from his wetness, and from the effects of punching-in with a pen-knife a beetle which had visited his tympanum, I began seriously to seek some means of exploring the northern head of the Tanganyika." On the one hand, Burton is dismissing pain as an inconvenience, no more than a footnote; on the other, he is laughing at Speke's damp ignominy, his frantic effort to overcome the invading beetle, and the failure of his mission.[13]

The critical moment came, however, with the decision that Speke should go by himself in search of the northern lake. Burton says he wanted to be rid of Speke's company, later writing the words, "to get rid of him," in the margins of his copy of *What Led* .... Lovell does not regard Burton's eagerness as surprising: "Under normal circumstances, as leader, Richard had nothing to lose; the results of an expedition—whichever team member makes the discoveries—are, after all, a group achievement." But circumstances were already anything but normal, and the rage to explore is a rage to possess.[14] If Burton could not have anticipated events as they turned out, he nonetheless had reason to be wary. What persuaded him to allow, or to encourage, an unmistakable threat to his prerogative?[15]

What kept him from travelling north, Burton claims, is that he had "other and more important matter to work out," namely, to gather geographical and other material from his Arab informants about tribes and kingdoms to the north, especially Uganda, whose despotic ruler Suna, with his harem of 3000 souls ("concubines, slaves and children"), captured Burton's imagination. Gather information he certainly did and Speke, he says, would have been in the way. It is in this context that we first learn of Speke's contempt for dark-skinned peoples: "his presence at Kazeh was by no means desirable. To associate at the same time with Arabs and Anglo-Indians, who are ready to take offence when it is least intended, who expect servility as their due, and whose morgue of colour"—their haughty superiority—"induces them to treat all skins a shade darker than their own as 'niggers,' is even more difficult than to avoid a rupture when placed between two friends who have quarrelled with each other." This is the original, then, of Burton on Speke's Anglo-Indian attitudes, attitudes here supposed to justify the puzzling decision to let Speke go off without him. Speke wins the prize of the Nile because his racial attitudes would have obstructed Burton's ethnographic and geographical inquiries. If the story happens to be true, the irony is palpable.[16]

Was it true? Speke had claimed in *Blackwood's* that Burton was "most unfortunately, quite done up" and needed to "recruit his health." In *What Led . . .* he eventually refashioned the story in a way that burnished his own image, Burton's failing health providing him the chance to be magnanimous: "I said, If you are not well enough when we reach Kazé I will go by myself, and you can employ the time in taking notes from the travelled Arabs of all the countries round." Burton is not likely to have told Speke outright that his presence would impede research, much less that the problem lay in Speke's Anglo-Indian attitudes. In his anxiety to be rid of his companion, however, Burton might have said something like "I'm quite done up, go along without me." If so, Speke would be reporting in *Blackwood's* what he believed were true facts, and then enhancing them in *What Led* . . . so as to give himself the lead role. And, under the smart of having lost the game, Burton's pointing to Speke's racism as a hindrance to his research may also have a basis in fact. Not that Speke's presence would have been incompatible in any serious way with research into such matters, all reported in *The Lake Regions*, as the rainy season in the hills of Karagwe (now a northwestern district of Tanzania), the price of coffee, or the very grand names assumed by Suna, the despot of Uganda. In gathering such data, Burton might have found Speke's presence a nuisance but surely not disabling. And, as commanding officer, he could have diminished the nuisance by sending Speke off to shoot game (even granting that game was scarce near Kazeh and ammunition supplies low) or by setting him tasks necessary for their return to the coast.[17]

Yet there may be another reason why Burton desired Speke's absence—a reason linked to the embarrassment of Speke's Anglo-Indian "morgue" and more compelling than the demands of research into the rainfall in Karagwe or the price of coffee. Possibly Burton's research engaged him in activities that Speke's Anglo-Indian mind would have found distasteful, and here the question of Burton's sexual interests turns up again, not only his own propensities but, more to the point, his curiosity about the practices of others.

On the matter of his own tastes, Brodie and Lovell have argued Burton's homosexuality, Brodie for the affirmative; Lovell, the negative. But evidence is scant and circumstantial. Brodie's argument depends on "Burton's passion for the forbidden," his "periodic but close association with sexually marginal characters," and "foremost in importance . . . [,] the Karachi episode, for one must doubt that a young man of twenty-four could make an intensive study of a male brothel without some degree of participation. Most men would flee from such an assignment in disgust." Lovell's argument depends on Burton's long marriage and "a great deal of previously unpublished material which demonstrates that Burton was heterosexual, and that prior to his successful marriage he had a number of heterosexual affairs ... and that he loved Isabel in the romantic sense." To Lovell, one can answer, case not proven, if only because we no longer attach conclusive meaning to the terms "homosexual" and "heterosexual." To Brodie, one can answer analogously. Whatever can or cannot be demonstrated, Burton probably had homosexual as well as heterosexual experiences and, in this, would not have been much different from many an English male of the time—though possibly different from John Hanning Speke.[18]

Speke must have been aware of Burton's sexual appetites, whatever they were, before they ever reached Kazeh, and they are not likely to have been the chief reason why Burton sent him off to the north. A more urgent motive might have been Burton's ongoing research into sexual customs, research that may have intersected in ways we cannot know with his own practices. There had been his report on the Karachi brothels. There had been his description of circumcision in the narrative of his pilgrimmage to Medina and Mecca. Soon there would be his trip to Salt Lake City, there to investigate the Mormon custom of polygamy—and to look "in vain for the outhouse-harems" in which he had heard, falsely, that "wives are kept, like any other stock." And, notoriously, there was his account (in Latin) of infibulation in Somaliland, intended as an appendix to *First Footsteps* but suppressed before publication, with its graphic description of intercourse between husband and a wife whose labia have been sewn: "at night when he goes to bed with his newly-wed bride [he] will strain to break through the blockage with his sword of love"—an ordinary metaphor though worth notice, coming from the great swordsman. "Generally he is unsuccessful; then he will attack this artificial hymeneal membrane with his finger. If he cannot overcome its defences by this method, he opens the pudendum from the lower end with a knife and immediately thrusts his penis up through the bloody opening. The pain is so intense as to cause the woman to shriek; to counteract this, male and female musicians drown the cries of the bride by singing . . . ." How did Burton gain his knowlege? If he wanted to investigate any such local practices in Kazeh, Speke would have been a very considerable nuisance.[19]

Still, coming back full circle, perhaps Burton *was* too sick to want to travel as well as sick of Speke's company and anxious to get on with his research. Perhaps he also thought that Speke was not likely to succeed in his quest. After all, he had not located the Wadi Nogal nor managed to acquire a dhow to explore Lake Tanganyika. Why should he succeed this time? When Speke returned from the northern lake, neither damp nor chagrined but proudly announcing he had found the source of the Nile, Burton must have been stunned—and also had some premonition of the misfortunes that were to fly forth from the Pandora's box he had opened.

He responded, in *The Lake Regions,* with anger, sarcasm, contempt, and a deluge of geographical reasons why Speke must be mistaken. But when confronted first in Kazeh with Speke's sunny optimism about what he had found, Burton could not have had at hand nor in his head all the data he would eventually marshal. His belief that Speke simply could not be right was as instinctive and self-regarding as Speke's intuition itself. Surely this mere English sportsman, with no previous successes to his credit, shaky credentials as a geographer, and no linguistic skills, could not have won the prize. Could he?

"On the morning of the 25ᵗʰ August," Burton reports, "reappeared my companion," his "flying trip" having taken him successfully to the northern lake, where "he had found its dimensions surpassing our most sanguine expectations." Burton maintains his role as leader: the expectations are "ours" rather than "his." But then: "We had scarcely, however, breakfasted, before he announced to me the startling fact, that he had discovered the sources of the White Nile." It is a familiar sport, to find moments in the past when one would like to have been present. Remembering the arid landscape around Kazeh (now Tabora), whistling acacias, scrubby trees, sometimes a baobab, I imagine a camp with tents; Burton in the process of making ready "a little expedition . . . to the southern provinces"; sounds of a caravan approaching; Burton's welcome to his companion, then tea and porridge or, possibly, even a grand breakfast like one that Speke describes in *What Led* . . . , "cold meat, potted Tanganyika shrimps, shrimp, rozelle jelly, with other delicacies, and coffee"; and—then—Speke says: "Dick, I've found it." Burton, incredulous. Or was he, at first, just sceptical? What a moment to have savored.[20]

Speke's intuitive certainty that he had found the source of the Nile seemed to Burton weakly grounded and womanish. "It was an inspiration perhaps," and inspiration is unworthy of the manly, scientific geographer: "the fortunate discoverer's conviction was strong; his reasons were weak" and of the sort "alluded to by the damsel Lucetta when justifying her penchant in favour of the 'lovely gentleman,' Sir Proteus:—

'I have no other but a woman's reason.
I think him so because I think him so.'"

While on their journey, the travellers had carried with them volumes of Shakespeare, of Euclid, "and so forth," and these volumes they read "together again and again." Among Shakespeare's plays, did they read *Two Gentlemen of Verona*—in which Julia's waiting woman Lucetta counsels her mistress on the merits of her suitors? Did Burton, like a learned schoolmaster, read aloud to his student-apprentice, or did they take turns? Play different roles? Burton's allusion to Lucetta's womanish reasoning, however pointed, is also oddly touching, even nostalgic, given what the travellers shared on their journey. And it is laced with irony: Lucetta, relying on womanly intuition, prefers Sir Proteus and she is right—just as Speke was right to think he had found the source of the Nile. Either Burton has an inkling that Speke might have beeen correct, or he does not notice that Lucetta's example is not exactly the one he requires.[21]

Things were very strained on the trek back to the coast and thence to Zanzibar: "After a few days it became evident to me that not a word could be uttered upon the subject of the Lake, the Nile, and his *trouvaille* generally without offence." The long trek, filled with arguments about what route to take and about payments to porters, all filling in for the real substance of the struggle, must have been painful for both travellers.[22]

Speke v. Burton

The sequence of texts relating to the expedition to the lakes bears recapitulation. First into the field was Speke with his articles in *Blackwood's*, September, October, and November, 1859: the first, entitled "Journal of a Cruise on the Tanganyika Lake;" the second and third, together, "Captain J. H. Speke's Discovery of the Victoria Nyanza Lake, the Supposed Source of the Nile." Then, early in 1860, while in Cape Town with Grant on their way to confirm the Nile source, Speke published *My Second Expedition to Eastern Intertropical Africa*, covering the early days of the expedition, and not included in *Blackwood's*, probably for want of compelling material. Why Speke published in Cape Town is uncertain but perhaps to raise money for the new expedition on which he and Grant were then embarked. It is unlikely that Burton ever saw a copy of *My Second Expedition*; and if he did, he would have found nothing other than Speke's Anglo-Indian morgue of color to disquiet him. Then, later in 1860, came Burton's tardily-appearing *The Lake Regions*, the book he had hoped to publish immediately on his return. Had he been able to beat Speke into print, we can assume he would have treated him as even more of a minor player than he did. We can also assume he would have tried to cement his prerogative to future exploration in East Africa, the prerogative that he thought Speke had stolen from him. The last act in this battle of texts then came in 1864 with Speke's *What Led to the Discovery of the Source of the Nile*, a sequel to his *Journal of the Dis-*

covery of the Source of the Nile, a text to which a whole team of Blackwood editors had played midwife.[23] In *What Led* . . . , Speke assembled,
with revisions, *My Second Expedition* and his three articles from *Blackwood's* into a single volume, joined together with his earlier adventures
in Somaliland. He therefore had the choice in *What Led* . . . of escalating
the quarrel or letting things stand as they were. In the event, he did not
dramatically change the *status quo*, but neither did he let slip some
chances to challenge Burton further, especially in his account of how he
happened to go alone to the Victoria Nyanza. His most dramatic response, however, is in a discrete, eight-page addition to the text that was
printed up by his publisher and bound into at least three surviving
copies of the volume, two for Speke himself, the third for his brother.[24]
Before coming to these remarkable pages, we should sample some of
Speke's less consequential differences with Burton, as they turn up in
the texts.

Did he (for example) return to Ujiji all wet and bedraggled? Both in
Blackwood's and then in *What Led* . . . , Speke tells the story otherwise—
and he could not, when he published in *Blackwood's*, have known how
Burton would tell it. About his failure to obtain a dhow, Speke is both
frank and contrite: "We arrived at Ujiji by breakfast-time, when I dis-
closed to Captain Burton, then happily a little restored, the mortifying
intelligence of my failing to procure the dhow. This must have been
doubly distressing to him, for he had been led to expect it by Khamis
[an Arab trader with whom they had travelled]." But he arrives in camp
in fair weather. Storms had almost swamped his boat a few days before,
indeed drenching him through, and the bad weather had gone on for
another day, making everything "wet and comfortless." But the day preceding his return is sunny—and "hailed with delight." A sunny day of
trekking is long enough to have warmed up and dried out and not arrived at Ujiji in the desolate condition Burton ascribes to him. Speke
has the better of things here. Not knowing that Burton would paint his
return in comic hues, he has no reason to play loose with facts. Maybe

Burton even took an unfair hint from Speke's own self-description as "wet and comfortless" in the days leading up to his return. All was fair in this love-war.[25]

Some amendments that Speke makes to the printed text of *My Second Expedition* in *What Led . . .* are designed to reflect badly on Burton. In *My Second Expedition,* an entry for February 10, 1857, reads: "Next morning, after following up the nullah for some considerable distance, we lit upon the rest of the party, sitting by a chain of pools, where they had bivouacked like ourselves; and, mingling together, commenced the march. At this time it was discovered that the surveying compass had been left behind, and I wished to return at once; but as no one would wait to show me the road, the instrument was abandoned." In *What Led . . .* the first sentence and opening phrases of the second are repeated, but "as no one would wait to show me the road" becomes: "as Captain Burton was knocked up, and would not wait for me, the instrument was abandoned." Leaving a surveying compass behind seems a reckless thing to do. Leaving it behind because the leader of the expedition is "knocked up"—tired and impatient to get on with the journey—is, if true, incriminating. Burton comes off as a less sturdy and less responsible voyager than his subordinate.[26]

Later in February, the travellers were on their way back to Zanzibar after exploring the coast and coastal towns as they waited for the rains to abate before tackling the interior. On February 16, in *My Second Expedition,* ". . . we came down to the Pangani"—a river that flows several hundred miles from the highlands near Kilimanjaro to the coast—"and in three days' travelling along it, put up once more at Kohodé, with Sultan Momba." The equivalent passsage in *What Led . . .* reads: ". . . we came down to the Pangani; and in three days' travelling along it, as Captain Burton, being no sportsman, would not stop for shooting, we put up once more at Kohodé, with Sultan Momba." The travellers sometimes squabbled for little more than the sake of squabbling. Speke wants to stop for shooting, Burton doesn't, and Speke is annoyed that his companion is "no sportsman." Perhaps being no sportsman is a moral failing because being a sportsman was an important part of being English. This is what Speke has thought from the start.[27]

But it is the decision that he should travel north from Kazeh by himself that inspires Speke's largest-scale revisions from the story as he had told it in *Blackwood's*. In rescripting the event, he gives himself the dominant role: Burton is languid, not eager to sustain new hardships. Speke has wanted to explore Lake Tanganyika further, but we learn in *What Led . . .* , for the first time, that Burton dragged his heels: "Captain Burton declared he would not, as he had had enough of canoe travelling, and thought our being short of cloth, and out of leave, would be sufficient excuse for him." Then, on the way back to Kazeh, Speke urges an expedition to the northern lake. What was, in *Blackwood's*, a cool proposal—"I then proposed that, after reaching Kazeh, we should travel northwards, in search of a lake, said by the Arabs to be both broader and longer than the Tanganyika"—becomes in *What Led . . .* a consuming desire: "I then proposed that, after reaching Kazé, we should travel northwards to the lake described by the Arabs to be both broader and longer than the Tanganyika. . . . I was all the while burning to see it." And, while Burton's response in *Blackwood's* is "graciously" to consent, in *What Led . . .* it is sullen lassitude—"Captain Burton at first demurred. He said we had done enough, and he would do no more"—followed by reluctant acquiescence when Speke plays the magnanimity card: he "finally gave way when I said, If you are not well enough when we reach Kazé I will go by myself, and you can employ the time in taking notes from the travelled Arabs of all the countries round. This was agreed to at last by Captain Burton. . . ."[28]

Not only does Speke take on the dominant role in his rewrite but now Burton plays the spoiler, refusing to let one of their Arab guides and informants, Sheikh Said, accompany Speke on his trek to the north. In *Blackwood's*, it is Said who is reluctant to go along: "The Shaykh demurred, saying he would give a definite answer about accompanying me before the time of starting, but subsequently refused (I hear, as one reason), because he did not consider me his chief." In *What Led . . .* , Speke explains in a note who was really to blame: "Sheikh Said has since declared"—presumably during the expedition with Grant—" 'in the most solemn manner, that Captain Burton positively forbade his going.' This happened . . . immediately after I first asked the Sheikh."[29] Speke also reports what Burton told him, that he "wanted to keep" Said with him "as he was a great friend of all the Arabs, and could procure him news better than any one else." Whatever lay behind Burton's reluctance, whether a desire for intelligence or a desire to impede Speke, the result was unfortunate. For July 10, 1858, Speke's entry reads, in *Blackwood's*, "The bad example set by Shaykh Said in shirking from this journey, is distressingly evident in every countenance. The Belooches"— Arab guards—"gloomy, dejected, discontented, and ever grumbling, form as disagreeable a party as was ever the unfortunate lot of any man to command." The entry in *What Led . . .* , otherwise the same as in *Blackwood's*, deletes any mention of Sheikh Said's "bad example." Burton alone is now at fault.[30]

But the notes that Speke attaches to the narrative in *What Led . . .* and other such changes seem almost trifling when set beside the new and startling evidence that he introduced in the eight pages prepared for but not printed in the text as first published. This evidence throws the story of his betrayal into question. He had a tale to tell, entirely different from Burton's, of what happened when the two parted company in Aden and Speke returned to England—and to the inner chambers of Sir Roderick Murchison and the Royal Geographical Society.

Betrayal?

What we know for certain is that Speke left Aden before his companion and, having arrived in London on May 8, 1859, went to see Murchison. Burton arrived a fortnight later. By then Speke had gained

Murchison's support for a return expedition, together with his easy-going Scottish friend, James Augustus Grant, to confirm the question of the Nile. Unhappy with this turn of events, Burton finished *The Lake Regions*, sent it to his publishers in April 1860, then left for North America and the Mormon world of Salt Lake City. By Christmas 1860, he was back in England. Speke and Grant were already well into their journey.

As happened at Kazeh, when Speke left to seek the northern lake, Burton seems to have miscalculated badly. But again, why and how? The story as told by Burton's biographers is one of Speke's betrayal. As told by Speke's biographer, it is one of weakness and the unlucky influence of others. Neither story may be true. Taken all together, the meta-story is about the reliability of facts, the interpretation of evidence, the shock of new information, and the way historical narratives become so deeply inscribed as to achieve the standing of accepted truth when they are only, at best, probable.

Among the numerous biographies of Burton in recent years, perhaps the best-known are by Byron Farwell, Fawn Brodie, and Mary Lovell. Each gives a somewhat different account of Burton's reasons for not leaving Aden with Speke. But each assumes Speke's betrayal, using one irresistible piece of evidence, the travellers' parting conversation.[31] That conversation comes from Burton's pen.

In Farwell, Burton merely "pleads" illness: he is tired of Speke's company and wants to be with his friend Dr. Steinhaeuser:

> Burton decided to leave Zanzibar on 22 March, taking a ship for Aden. He and Speke arrived there on 16 April and were greeted by Burton's old friend John Steinhaeuser. When HMS *Furious* came into port a few days later, the two explorers were offered transportation back to England. Speke left, but . . . Burton failed to hurry back for his reward. He pleaded illness, although Aden was certainly not the place for recuperation and a sea voyage generally had a good effect upon his health. Undoubtedly, the truth was that he simply wanted to be free of the companionship of Speke and to stay awhile with his friend Steinhaeuser.

Farwell signals that all is not so transparent as he would like: "undoubtedly" is often the biographer's recourse in moments of doubt.[32]

Then Farwell records Burton's famous story, as it was to become, of the final conversation.

> According to Burton, the following conversation was the last he ever had with Speke:
> Burton: 'I shall hurry up, Jack, as soon as I can.'
> Speke: 'Good-bye, old fellow. You may be quite sure I shall not go up to the Royal Geographical Society until you come to the fore and we appear together. Make your mind easy about that.'

The fact that Burton is the source of the conversation is carefully made, but is also casual, a detail in passing.[33]

Unlike Farwell, Brodie believes Burton really was extremely ill. Like Farwell, she repeats the parting conversation, irresistible fodder for the biographic imagination. She specifies the source of the conversation at the end of her account and without emphasis:

> On March 22, 1859, Burton and Speke boarded the clipper *Dragon of Salem* and sailed for Aden. There Burton met his trusted friend, Dr. John Steinhaeuser, who after talking privately with Speke went to Burton in alarm and warned him he would have trouble with Speke in London. Still the two explorers were exchanging formal courtesies, and were to outward appearances friends. But when H.M.S. *Furious* sailed into the Aden harbor en route to London, and they were offered passage, Burton declined. Steinhaeuser had urged him to convalesce a little longer in Aden. Fever still clung to him, Burton wrote, 'like the shirt of Nessus . . . .' The two explorers exchanged a brief goodbye. "I shall hurry up, Jack, as soon as I can," Burton said.
> And Speke replied, "*Goodbye old fellow; you may be quite sure I shall not go up to the Royal Geographical Society until you come to the fore and we appear together. Make your mind quite easy about that.*"
> "They were the last words," Burton wrote, "Jack ever spoke to me on earth."

The attribution of these "last words" to Burton would be easy for an inattentive reader to miss.[34]

Finally, Mary Lovell, whose account is fuller and more circumstantial. She too thinks that Burton was sick and that Steinhaeuser withheld a medical certificate for none other than medical reasons. And, like a moth to the inevitable flame, she flies to the final conversation—noting that Burton "recorded" the exchange:

> ... [A]waiting their arrival at Aden was Dr John 'Styggins' Steinhaueser, who had invited both men to stay at his home. On seeing Richard's condition he refused to give him a medical certificate to travel further, recommending immediate rest and nursing. A P. & O. steamer was due to leave Aden for London only twelve days later, but Speke decided not to wait. He went directly aboard the *Furious*, after a hurried farewell with Burton who recorded their final conversation. Speke, he stated, 'voluntarily promised, when reaching England, to visit his family in the country, and to await my arrival that we might appear together before the Royal Geographical Society.'
>
> Confident that he would be able to persuade Steinhaueser to give him a medical certificate in time for the next ship, Richard told Speke: 'I shall hurry up, Jack, as soon as I can.' To which Speke replied, 'Goodbye old fellow; you may be sure I shall not go up to the Royal Geographical Society until you come to the fore and we appear together. Make your mind quite easy about that.'

These parting words, by now the stuff of legend, are the foundation on which belief in Speke's betrayal rests.[35]

Alexander Maitland, a young man when he published *Speke* in 1971, reports the conversation more as a mark of continued amity, however strained, between the explorers than as calculated deceit. But repeat it he does: ". . . [I]n their brief adieus, neither Burton nor Speke betrayed the least suspicion of declining confidence in each other and . . . , on the contrary, Burton's last words were full of optimism while Speke spontaneously offered his hand in friendship and reassurance. Said Burton, 'I shall hurry up, Jack, as soon as I can.' To which Speke answered 'Goodbye old fellow . . . .'" And so on. In the mythology of African exploration, only "Dr. Livingstone, I presume," is better known or more enduring.[36]

Until now, Burton has been our only source of information about the parting in Aden. He touches on it three times: in *The Lake Regions*, expressing indignation at Speke's actions after his "spontaneous offer;" in the valedictory "Captain Speke," adding that Speke intended, on reaching England, "to visit his family in the country" to await Burton's arrival; and in the journal recorded by Isabel in her biography, where the legendary conversation itself appears for the first time: "When H.M.S. *Furious*, carrying Lord Elgin and Mr. Laurence Oliphant, his secretary, arrived at Aden, passage was offered to both of us. I could not start, being too ill. But *he* went, and the words Jack said to me, and I to him, were as follows . . . ." We know by now what those words were. Is there any reason to be suspicious, even leaving aside any new evidence?[37]

At least it is possible to think about them anew. In a novel with an unembroidered title, *Burton and Speke* (1982), William Harrison recognizes the texture and tone of the conversation:

> 'Take care,' Speke said.
> 'I shall hurry up, Jack, as soon as I can,' Burton replied.
> 'Goodbye, old fellow,' Speke then said, clearing his throat. He seemed to have prepared a speech and appeared nervous in delivering it. 'You may be quite sure. . . .'

Harrison is right: the speech has the feel of tinned goods, just what a very English explorer might be thought to have said to his un-English companion. But need that mean, as Harrison assumes, that the stiffness of the words indicates a premeditated lie? Probably so—*if* Speke actually spoke them as reported. But did he? We have no authority besides Burton or, perhaps, none besides Isabel, whose chaotic rag-bag of a biography is stuffed with "scattered letters, cuttings, extracts, etc., at random in nearly every chapter, thus turning the 'Life' into a Burtonian scrap-book" (as Norman Penzer accurately describes it). Among the extracts are some 70 pages, headed "Zanzibar; and Two Months in East

Africa" and described by Isabel as "from his own notes." These pages include much about the Tanganyika expedition that Burton had printed in *The Lake Regions* and much about Speke that he had not, including their parting words. The description of these pages as "from his own notes" creates a presumption of their primacy. Yet they do not claim to be original and untouched. Their exact relationship, temporal and otherwise, to the composition of *The Lake Regions* is beyond reconstruction. But, like *The Lake Regions*, they are put together after the fact. A fair question is, how long after?[38]

To that question, we have one good answer: the famous conversation was recorded—or composed—more than five years later than those parts of Burton's text that appear both in *The Lake Regions* and in Isabel's biography. So far as I am aware, this has not previously been noticed. But it is the inescapable conclusion when one looks at the text anew: "the words Jack said to me, and I to him, were as follows:—'I shall hurry up, Jack, as soon as I can,' and the last words Jack ever spoke to me on earth were, *'Good-bye, old fellow; you may be quite sure I shall not go up to the Royal Geographical Society until you come to the fore and we appear together. Make your mind quite easy about that.'*" The italics stand out. Only Brodie among the biographers reproduces them, along with a note stating that "the italics are Burton's." But Isabel was fond, even enamored, of italics; perhaps these are not Burton's but hers. A second thing stands out: the conversation is reported at length—and verbatim. Third, and most important, Burton announces he is recording "the last words Jack ever spoke to me on earth." Therefore he is writing sometime after Speke's death in September, 1864 (unless, as seems very unlikely, he recorded the words earlier and later inserted the claim that they were the "last words Jack ever spoke to me"). It would require a major suspension of disbelief to think that words Burton thus reports verbatim, years after they were supposedly uttered, could be more than an approximation of what was actually said. And there is reason to guess that Burton's recreation is inflected by a memory of Speke's normal style. The man who utters this farewell is the virtual parody of a comic Englishman, someone who could have been invented by Kingsley Amis. This does not mean Speke's parting speech is unlike him—on the contrary, it is probably quite like him—but that is not to say we need accept it at face value.[39]

The pre-cooked quality of the final conversation, as it is reported by Burton, carries over to his own words, too. " 'I shall hurry up, Jack, as soon as I can' " is in the same hearty English-country-squire style as " 'Good-bye old fellow; you may be sure . . .' " and the exchange reads like a small, colonial playlet—one reason, no doubt, why it has been so universally accepted. It is not hard to suppose, however, that Burton, with his mastery of languages and his penchant for disguise, could have created the dialogue, maybe even without full consciousness of being inventive, so as to capture a tone. Having reported in *The Lake Regions* that Speke spontaneously gave an undertaking not to go to the Royal Geographical Society without him, Burton has the basis on which to invent or re-imagine what he and Speke had said. The last conversation has the same liabilities as any dialogue reconstructed well after the fact. Its truth status is uncertain.

But why, one might have asked in 1864, did Speke not respond to the charge that he had freely offered to await Burton's arrival in London? And now, it remarkably turns out, he did respond, though in a manner so curious as to deepen the puzzle further. At this point, the story turns into the genre that Robert Altick calls the scholarly thriller. One of Altick's tales, so engaging as to deserve recall, will serve as an introit. A hopeful biographer of George Eliot and G. H. Lewes, Anna Kitchel, was in London, having come up with little new material. While riding in a bus, she told a companion seated next to her of her disappointment. At that point "the woman in the seat ahead turned and quietly asked, 'Would you care to see George Lewes's diaries?' " Serendipity, as Altick says, is as important as diligence. The tale of how Speke's response came into sight—or at least into my sight—is not quite a case of sitting behind the right person on the right bus, but it is a story of some very good luck indeed.[40]

In the winter of 2004, Christie's auction house announced an upcoming sale in London of travel books and manuscripts belonging to the late Quentin Keynes. The catalogue, when it arrived, was sumptuous and the material—Burton, Speke, Livingstone, Stanley, and many others, most of African interest—dazzling. Of the five hundred lots to be sold, lot 471, "Speke's Copy of the First Edition" of *What Led to the Discovery of the Source of the Nile*, "Corrected by Him and With Additional Corrected Text," was the stunner, though the catalogue entry left much to wonder about. The corrections were said to be "in preparation for a proposed second edition which was never published." The "additional" text extended the narrative by eight pages, "continuing Speke's story until his arrival in England in April 1859." This extension, in turn, Speke mentions in a letter—included in the same lot—to George Simpson of Blackwood's, manager of the firm's Edinburgh office. The letter is dated August 18, 1864. In it Speke tells Simpson: " 'The ladies all like the tail and with myself cannot see what more harm it could do than other parts contained in the body of the work, whilst all equally say the best policy is the [*sic*] "speak the truth, and shame the Devil." ' " All this information is in the catalogue. Was there ever a more intriguing entry? Was the eight page extension, "the tail," typeset or in manuscript? What did it contain?[41]

I set out on a trail that included any number of phone calls to London in the early morning hours, California time, incurring obligations that I have acknowledged elsewhere; without the help of others this story could not have been told—or not, at least, here. Miraculously, the venerable firm of Maggs Brothers had recently sold a copy of *What Led . . .* , originally owned by Speke, who presented it to his aunt, that also contained the additional eight pages; my first knowledge of what these pages were and what they contained came from information regarding the Maggs copy. The pages are printed text, continuously paginated as 373–380, and bound in after page 372, which carries the words, as in other copies originally printed, "THE END." Pages 373–380 are unquestionably "the tail" that all the ladies like—Speke's three sisters, we can assume, and his mother, Georgina, to whom he extended a large measure of filial devotion. In a letter to Norton Shaw, April 15, 1860, he congratulated himself on his mother's approval of James Grant, soon to accompany him on his return to the lakes: " 'Mother thinks no end of our friend Grant and is immensely pleased with the idea of my having such a good companion.' " Georgina's opinion mattered to her son, and she played an active part in his affairs. In 1861, troubled by the prospect of a disagreeable public "altercation," she prevailed with Blackwood not to publish an early version of *What Led* . . . , including material Speke had sent from Africa when he learned of "some bitter things" Burton had said about him in *The Lake Regions.* So strongly was the family opposed to an unseemly public quarrel, Georgina told Blackwood, that they wished "to put it out of [Hanning's] power." If Speke is reporting the opinion of "the ladies" fairly, however, things had come to such a pass by August 1864 that Georgina and his sisters could agree that time had come to speak the truth and shame the devil—and his latter-day avatar, Richard Burton.[42]

For information concerning the Quentin Keynes copy, its likely provenance and its contents, and for the story of the eight extra pages, I have incurred further obligations, also acknowledged elsewhere. Evidently the additional pages were printed at the same time as the original text and bound into at least three copies, one for Speke himself, another for presentation to his aunt, and a third that his brother Ben presented to a friend. In August, a few months after publication, Speke then sent his copy back to George Simpson in Edinburgh, with emendations throughout, including several on the final eight pages, all in anticipation of a second edition that would have included "the tail." When Speke died in September, plans for a second edition were scrapped. The amended copy would have remained in the vast Blackwood archive until it was purchased by Quentin Keynes, probably at a public sale in the second half of the twentieth century, then to be sold again after Keynes's death. These eight pages include a radically new version of what happened in Aden when Speke and Burton parted company.

It will be useful first to sample the whole eight pages, all of them having come now into public view, before turning to Speke's account of the parting in Aden. "In a few words more," he begins, "I shall briefly describe how the expedition came out of Africa, and what became of the men who brought us safely to the end of our journey." There follows a narrative of incompatibility and internecine bickering: "my companion would not listen to any further protraction of the journey" (Speke had proposed a more ambitious route back to Zanzibar than the one Burton preferred); "Captain Burton, on the other hand, said . . ."; "Captain Burton, however, wanted their protection"—that of slaves owned by an Indian trader—"but did not want to pay them"; "I begged my companion to leave me and travel to the coast by himself, as I preferred being alone to being a drag on him"—Speke is "thoroughly prostrated" by "an attack of the lungs"—"but he would not hear of it, saying he feared the rebukes his friends might cast on him if he abandoned me"; "Captain Burton would not listen to this . . ."; and "Captain Burton did not like the idea of any more roughing on shore." Even Burton's reluctance to abandon a sick companion depends less on his good will than on his fear of being rebuked by friends.[43]

Only at the end do we arrive at the devil-shaming truth that, if it happens to be true, overturns Burton's story. Speke lets drop his version off-handedly. Having arrived at Aden, he is still brooding about Burton's reluctance to pay their guides: "With a heavy heart I wrote back to Rigby on behalf of the men who had brought us through the journey, and begged him to see them righted, for I thought if they were not, no travellers would ever again be able to enter the country, and our having gone there would have had a most prejudicial effect." And then, the shock: "I did this in a hurry, because Captain Burton said he would not go to England for many months, as he intended to go to Jerusalem. My surmise was justified . . ."[44]

Now, without a pause for breath, Speke reports, as proof of his surmise about the experience of future travellers, the failure of another expedition at "about the time my letter reached Zanzibar . . . simply because the white man was feared as a master."[45] Then Burton is suddenly out of sight and mind. Speke's passage home on the *Furious* is a fair-weather cruise: "a more delightful one I never experienced." And then, another shock: "a fortnight after my landing in England, Captain Burton unexpectedly arrived." Once again Speke moves on, hardly pausing for breath: "we were required by the Royal Geographical Society each to lecture one night in their rooms—he on the ethnology of the countries we had travelled, and I on the geography." In his lecture, Speke "for the first time, propounded in public my opinion that the Victoria N'yanza would eventually prove to be the source of the Nile." This is all breathtaking. Burton's arriving "unexpectedly" in England is passed off, without a tremor, as just a prelude to their appearance at the Royal Geographical Society. Everything is in good working order, nothing in disarray—except the unexpectedness of Burton's return, and even that barely upsets the equilibrium. The calm is preternatural.[46]

More needs to be said, and will be, about these remarkable eight pages and about Speke's claim that Burton arrived in England unexpectedly. Enough evidence is now in sight, however, to pose the question, was John Hanning Speke the "cad" that some have believed him to be?

CHAPTER SIX

Was Speke a Cad?

It is Speke's very Englishness that solicits—if you believe he behaved badly—the Victorian epithet: a cad. Byron Farwell says: "Both Rigby and Grant have testified to Speke's modesty, but from his actions and his letters he certainly appears the reverse. The more one learns of Speke's character, the less wholesome it is revealed. It is difficult to escape the conclusion that the discoverer of the major source of the Nile and the largest lake in Africa was a cad." And members of the Royal Geographical Society, at the height of Speke's success, grew suspicious—the words are Fawn Brodie's—that he "was acting the cad." The charge of caddishness has stuck, and Alexander Maitland feels a need to answer, even at the price of casting his subject as easily swayed by others: "Speke was not the guilty 'cad' that several writers and commentators would have us believe. Rather, he was trusting, easily swayed by charm, and possessed of that comb of vanity which, if stroked gently and often, would so deprive him of all good judgement that he would temporarily forsake the path of reason for others alien and even quite disastrous." Following Isabel Burton's lead, Maitland believes that on his journey home from Aden to England, Speke fell under the sinister influence of Laurence Oliphant, then travelling with Lord Elgin, whom he had served as private secretary on Elgin's mission to China: "Oliphant was certainly efficient, although his motive is at first somewhat obscure . . . Left to himself, Speke would not have deliberately misled Burton, but would have faced him fair and square." In fact Oliphant's motive, assuming there is anything at all to the story, is obscure both at first and second glance, but he is a convenient scapegoat. Oliphant's biographer Anne Taylor, responding to Isabel's allegation and to a later allegation of a homosexual relationship between the two men, judges that "the truth of the matter seems likely to have been much less dramatic and much less damaging . . . When he met him on board *Furious* it is likely that Speke"—angry and exasperated with Burton—"found Laurence Oliphant no more than a sympathetic audience. . . ." But she does not doubt that Speke betrayed Burton and that Oliphant may have played some part.[1]

On the website devoted to Richard Burton, a graduate student from the United Kingdom recently posted a question about Speke: "This man was a complete and utter bounder. Discuss." "Complete and utter bounder" comes from the same semantic world as "cad." The first instance of "cad" in the *Oxford English Dictionary*, "a fellow of low vulgar manners and behaviour," is from 1838. Over time the meaning of cad ascended the social scale to refer to unprincipled members of the upper classes. The first instance of "bounder," "a person of objectionable manners or anti-social behaviour; a cad," is from 1889. Each epithet means something not far from "scoundrel"—in particular, a scoundrel whose behavior violates the normal standards of class. Each epithet balances, now, on the edge of being quaint, the structure of Victorian society having dissolved and been transformed. Cole Porter, in *Kiss Me Kate*, rhymes "Pad-u-a" with "what-a-cad-you-are." "Bounder" is fair material for farce. The graduate student who posted the proposition that Speke was "a complete and utter bounder" knew what she was doing. In 1876 (according to an entry in the *Oxford English Dictionary*), Max Beerbohm said: "It is the cadism of English residents in India which galls the natives"—a comment underscoring the social foundations behind the serio-comic questions: Was Speke a bounder? A cad?

Respondents to the student's question said, in general, no, Speke was not a bounder. Or not quite. One said: "No, [he was] just limited and probably no more than averagely caddish." Others said he was "terribly insecure," "very insecure and easily manipulated," "good at deluding himself." Oliphant and Rigby were bad influences: "Speke was probably alright until he came under the influence of Laurence Oliphant, who really was a complete and utter bounder;" "Oliphant really enjoyed mischief and was pleased seeing Burton taken down a peg or two"; and, "if you are really interested in individuals who encouraged Speke in his betrayal of Burton look into Rigby, who also hated Burton because of intellectual jealousy." The discussion reflects received opinion. These are knowledgeable students of Burton who want to be fair to his rival. History has assimilated Isabel Burton's claim of Oliphant's malign influence and Maitland's claim that Speke was easily swayed. Add the one to the other and they yield the proposition that Speke was "insecure"—an all-purpose explanation for many an infelicity of character and behavior. It is also an explanation that calls for an explanation.

Speke and Conflict

Speke did not enjoy conflict, a marker of his insecurity no doubt but also of his gentility. He did not like conflict even when he initiated or contributed greatly to it himself. He liked to be liked; or, at least, he did not like not to be liked. That is the conclusion to be drawn not only, and above all, from his relationship with Burton but also from his about-face in the case of Sumunter and from certain of his dealings with another—major—actor in the story, John Petherick, British consul at Khartoum, who offended him by not meeting him, as planned, at the moment when he and Grant arrived in Gondokoro, on the upper reaches of the Nile, after the expedition to locate the river's source. We have followed the curious story of Speke and Sumunter. We will come to the distressing story of Speke and Petherick. In each case, Speke sought to smooth over difficulties. With Burton and with Petherick, he seems not to have to understood that some things were as they were— not to be effaced by polite civilities.

In the months after Speke and Burton returned to England in May 1859, the air grew thick with acrimony. Burton disputed Speke's geography and his claim to the Nile. Speke made dismissive comments to Norton Shaw: "Burton is one of those men who never *can* be wrong, and will never acknowledge an error"; and, "I cannot help thinking what a green thing it was of Burton not remarking that when at Kazeh, we were due south of Gondokoro with a sea, according to everybodies account, stretching clear up to it. It is a devil of a bore having to go all over the same stale ground again." Burton's failure to have paid the expedition guards heightened the friction, and Speke's remonstrances to Rigby brought an official request to Burton that he explain what happened. Reacting furiously, Burton cut Speke dead when he met him at the Royal Geographical Society, leaving copies of the correspondence in view for members of the Society to read along with an open letter to Shaw that said, "I don't wish to have any further private or direct communication with Speke. At the same time I am anxious that no mention of his name by me should be made without his being cognizant of it." Knowing that Speke has been talking freely behind his back, Burton takes public revenge but manages an appearance of high-mindedness. Other money still owing for expedition expenses made matters worse. Speke wanted Burton to seek a refund from the government; Burton thought that would be useless and dunned Speke for his share, almost £750. By the time Speke was to leave for Africa in April 1860, the antagonism was acute.[2]

And, at that point, Speke made an overture of friendship. He wrote Burton a placatory letter, explaining that he couldn't lay hands on the money before leaving the country but had arranged for his brother to pay what was owing. Burton replied very formally. On April 16, only days before he and Grant were to set out, Speke wrote again to say the money would be available "immediately after the refusal has been received to refund you from the Gov't. Treasury." This final letter he addressed "My dear Burton"—contrasting with Burton's chilly "Sir." And he began, "I cannot leave England addressing you so coldly as you have hitherto been corresponding . . ." Burton's answer, which survives in a draft penned at the bottom of Speke's letter, was glacial: "Sir, I have received your note of the 16th April. With regard to the question of debts I have no objection to make. I cannot, however, accept your offer concerning our corresponding less coldly—any other tone would be extremely distasteful to me." This is the end of their correspondence.[3]

Mary Lovell judges Speke harshly in this last exchange: "Anyone who has researched this feud in depth will sympathise with Richard's response that while he accepted the financial terms he could not 'accept your offer concerning our corresponding less coldly.'" No one knows more about Burton's life than Lovell, who has quarried many an archive. The account I have given here, especially of events after Burton and Speke returned in 1859, draws heavily (and gratefully) on *A Rage to Live*. Yet Lovell's harsh view of Speke, at this last moment of communication between the voyagers, arises less from research than from partiality. Even though Speke was unrealistic to expect a less frigid response, he did what he could.[4]

Lovell also calls Speke's promise to pay his debt when the goverment has refused to cover it "an astonishing example of hypocrisy"—because he had recently learned from the India Office that a refund " 'was unlikely.' " But what is hypocritical in saying he will pay up when it becomes certain that no refund will be forthcoming? That is what many reasonable persons would do. If you owe a debt provisionally, but there remains some chance that the obligation will be covered, it is surely more prudent to wait until the matter is resolved, especially if you mistrust your fellow creditor. Speke's final overture to Burton is marked by the knowledge that he is soon to leave on a very long and dangerous voyage with an unpredictable outcome. Probably he has not forgotten the strange remark he made years before about coming to Africa to be killed. Probably he also wonders if this will be his last communication with his one-time friend. There are few things "not purely evil," Samuel Johnson said, "of which we can say, without some emotion of uneasiness, 'this is the last.'" The imminence of the last hangs in the air as Speke prepares to depart. Alexander Maitland describes his hope of reconciliation as "touching and sincere." We may wonder whether Burton ever sent the letter he drafted; if he did, whether it reached Speke before he left his family home on April 18; and, if he did receive it, what effect it had on him. He may have left for Africa in a disturbed state of mind.[5]

Petherick

The story of Speke's dealing with John Petherick has enhanced his reputation as a cad. He treated Petherick and his loyal, engaging, and intrepid wife, Kate, who travelled with him, both strangely and unpleasantly. All that might be offered in his defense is that he was, as with Oliphant, perhaps influenced by others. Either that or, by the end of his expedition with Grant, he was suffering from some measure of what Burton called "cerebral" impairment.

Having contracted with the Royal Geographical Society to meet Speke and Grant after their expedition and to provide them with transportation down river to Cairo, Petherick and his wife arrived in ample time to carry out the mission on schedule and arranged for boats and supplies to be made available in Gondokoro. But Speke and Grant did not show up for many months after they had been expected. In the meanwhile the Pethericks went exploring and trading; Petherick operated a station west of Gondokoro. They stayed in touch, however, to learn if word had been received of the travellers. Their contract with the Royal Geographical Society stated that, if the travellers did not arrive on schedule, they were not obliged to remain beyond June 1862. In the event, when they arrived in Gondokoro in February 1863, the Pethericks found that Speke and Grant had been waiting for five days—small reason, on the face of it, for Speke to take offence. But he did, very strenuously.

As Petherick describes it in *Travels in Central Africa* (1869), the late-arriving volume in which he eventually told his story and defended himself against his antagonists, Speke greeted him with unexpected hostility: "Instead . . . of the cordial meeting I had anticipated from the ardently sought-for, and now successful, travellers, we were met with coolness and a positive refusal to partake of more of our stores or assistance than would satisfy their most urgent requirements, and that elsewhere could not be obtained." And instead of proceeding to Khartoum in Petherick's boats, Speke elected to travel with boats offered him by Samuel Baker, another English explorer, who was in Gondokoro at the same time, not at all by chance. Petherick continues: "Without any intimation of his reasons for so doing, Speke immediately removed his effects from the 'Kathleen' "—a boat Petherick had provided—"and, in reply to my urgent solicitations that he should retain possession of her and accept of as many of the other boats as he wished, to proceed on his voyage down the Nile, he coolly replied, 'I do not wish to recognize the succour dodge, and friend Baker has offered me his boats.' " Since Speke and Petherick had mutually agreed on the plan that would take Petherick to Gondokoro and that the Royal Geographical Society had sanctioned, Speke's accusation that the Pethericks are engaged in some sort of "succour dodge" seems unaccountable. Something has gone terribly wrong. Whatever it may have been, Speke was reluctant to talk about it: he moved his effects from the Pethericks' boat to Baker's, giving no hint of his reasons.[6]

Kate Petherick tells her sister a similar story in a letter she wrote in the fall of 1863 and later incorporated in the narrative of *Travels in Central Africa*. She thought Baker had played an active and malicious part: " 'When at Gondokoro, I felt convinced that some treachery was work-

ing against Petherick, so I went to Baker's boat, and implored him . . .
not to offer his boats to Captain Speke, as he, Mr. Baker, well knew the
peculiar position Petherick held' "—the position afforded, presumably,
by his contract with the Royal Geographical Society—"and that he was
also aware that our boats had arrived prior to his." To this Baker replied,
"Oh, Mrs. Petherick, it will be a positive service to me if he goes to
Khartoum in my boats, as the men are paid in advance, and his will
serve as escort and guard." In the face of this politely vague answer, Kate
yields, "tearfully," her tears revealing how much, in this contest for re-
flected glory, is at stake. Supplies intended for Speke's use are packed up
but returned to the Pethericks with a note saying that Baker has provided what is needed. And then the travellers dine together, all supping
on a "tremendous ham" that the Pethericks, looking forward to the occasion, have brought from England. As much as I would like to have
shared the breakfast when Speke told Burton he had found the Nile, I
might choose instead, if given only a single choice, to join this dinner
over the enormous ham that the Pethericks had brought all the way
from England. The evening must have been ghastly. Kate writes: "During dinner, I endeavoured to prevail upon Speke to accept our aid, but
he drawlingly replied, 'I do not wish to recognize the succour dodge';
the rest of the conversation I am not well enough to repeat. I grow
heart-sick now, as I did then, after all our toil. Never mind, it will recoil
upon him yet, his heartless conduct." Might the reason for Speke's
heartlessness have been found somewhere in the conversation that Kate
Petherick feels not well enough to repeat? Since her letter goes on from
here, it cannot be physical ill-health that stops her pen. In any case, we
know that she holds Baker as well as Speke to blame: "Petherick, so honest and true himself, believes every one the same, and would not listen
to my fears that Speke and Baker wished us not well." Whatever went
wrong, Baker had a hand in it. Like Laurence Oliphant in the Speke-
Burton story, he is the mystery card.[7]

Not only did Speke treat Petherick maliciously at Gondokoro, he dealt severe blows to his reputation back in England, charging him with misuse of public funds, including £100 donated by Speke's father. But the most serious charge was that Petherick had been engaged in the slave trade. Speke made this allegation both privately in official quarters and at a public banquet in his honor. Petherick learned of what Speke said while he was laid up in Khartoum, suffering an infestation of parasitic worms "revelling in the fleshy part of my right leg and foot": "Whilst in this state, a paragraph from the 'Overland Mail' was placed in my hands, descriptive of a banquet in honour of Captain Speke on his return to Taunton. In that portion of his address touching upon the slave trade, he (as it was broadly stated in another paper) obviously referred to me when saying, 'men with authority emanating from our Government, who are engaged with the native kings in the diabolical slave trade.' My experience of Speke at Gondokoro, and also the tone of his last letter, written under my roof at Khartoum"—while Speke was on his way home and Petherick still in Gondokoro—"ill prepared me for so wilful an effusion of slander and calumny. The blow was as hard as I could well bear . . . ." Petherick is so upset that he decides to enter proceedings against Speke "at a future date." But "his subsequent deplorable death, while on my way home, unfortunately deprived me of this satisfaction." "Deplorable" is mildly startling: "deplorable" because it is to be lamented or only because it deprives Petherick of the chance to sue?[8]

Mary Lovell concludes that "Speke ruined Petherick's career just as he had previously severely damaged Burton"; and, it is true, Petherick lost his consulship in Khartoum in part because of Speke's charges. Amongst Lovell's evidence is a letter from Murchison to Austen Henry Layard, July 1, 1864, indicating how troubled and how troubling was Speke's state of mind. Murchison tells Layard: "Speke sent me telegrams from Paris"—in March 1864—"denouncing Petherick, but which I could not read or produce so intemperate were they. They are tied up and docketed with others as 'Speke's visions'! I have deeply regretted

these aberrations . . ." There can be no doubt that Speke was greatly dis-
tressed if Murchison maintained a file for his "visions." Is there anything, however, that might extenuate, if not excuse, his treatment of the
Pethericks?[9]

In the first place, rumors that Petherick was involved in the slave
trade did not originate with Speke. These allegations went back at least
four years, on Petherick's own account, to a report in April 1860 that the
Austrian Consular Agent in Khartoum, Joseph Natterer, sent to his
Consul-General in Alexandria. This report, as translated into French,
reached Petherick through the Foreign Office. It claimed that, while no
German or Austrian citizens were engaged in slaving, French traders,
one Englishman, and one Maltese were trafficking: "de toute le colonie
de Khartoum il n'y a que les Français, et de plus un Anglais, et un Mal-
tais, qui trafiquent d'esclaves, et se rendent coupables des actions honteuses donc je vient de parler." The Englishman could only have been
Petherick, who protested. On his request, Natterer explained in a letter
of March 1862 that his report had been mistranslated: "I beg to inform
you that in the translation of that report into French an unpleasant error has crept in. After I had described the bartering trade with the negro
populations as having suffered in consequence of the slave trade, I said
that the Germans were settled here in Khartoum, and that Frenchmen,
Italians, one Englishman, and one Maltese carried on *trade* upon the
White River. The translator has erroneously taken this to mean *slave
trade.* At that time I did not at all know who was carrying on the slave
trade on the White River, and therefore not the slightest imputation was
intended to be cast upon you, which fact I hereby acknowledge." The
eclipse of Petherick's career and reputation has largely cost him a place
in the historical record. Had he been less unlucky, we might by now
have a biography of him or at least an entry in the *Dictionary of National Biography.* And if we had a biography, perhaps the original of
Natterer's 1860 report would have come to light. We also might know
more about circumstances of the translation. As it is, we have to wonder

whether Natterer's abject explanation, solicited by Petherick, can be accepted at face value. If it was only trading, not slave trading, that he referred to, what can have been the shameful actions ("des actions honteuses") of the traders? And is a translator likely to have made so large a slip as to mistake ordinary trade for slaving?[10]

Petherick also reports having received a letter, delivered as he was trekking toward Gondokoro in February 1863, that Baker had written him after he arrived there on February 2. In it he thanks Petherick for his hospitality—" 'the hospitality of my roof during six months' stay at Khartoum.' " The main burden of the letter, however, is less agreeable. Accusations against Petherick have resurfaced and multiplied in Khartoum—the result, Baker says, of "irritation" over Petherick's arrest of two men for slave trading. As Baker tells it, " 'an accusation was sent to the Consul-General against you, signed by nearly all the Europeans at Khartoum, including the official declarations of the two Consulates' " —presumably those of France and Austria—" 'charging you with some former participation in slavery. Of course the seals of numerous natives ornamented the document.' " This report of some "former" participation in slavery, together with Speke's broadcasting of the charges, inspired Petherick in 1864 to seek assurance that his reputation was clear—and later to reproduce letters of exoneration from Theodore von Heuglin, "Court Councillor" for the state of Würtemberg; from G. Thibaut, representing the consulate of France; and from M. L. Hansal, representing the consulate of Austria. Like Natterer's two years before, these letters all absolve Petherick of slaving. Thibaut says: " 'I am astonished to learn that you have been accused of having carried on an illicit trade at Kordofan and on the White River. I can positively state that, having been for many years your neighbour in Kordofan, I have seen nothing in your conduct that would warrant such a defamation of character. Like an honest man you engaged in the regular trade of the produce of the country, such as gum and ivory.' " But if the consulates had in fact made "official declarations" linking Petherick to the slave trade, the same uneasy questions hang over these new testimonials as those over Natterer's claim that he had been mistranslated. Petherick mounts a passionate self-defense, however, not only saying that he intended to enter proceedings against Speke but asserting the "absurdity" of his having prosecuted others "in the event of my ever having exposed myself to a similar charge."[11]

Khartoum depended on the slave economy. "Any penniless adventurer," writes Alan Moorehead, "could become a trader," and the trade was what "kept Khartoum going." Officially it was illegal, "but the only effect of this was that the slaves were not sold openly in Khartoum . . . . Probably nothing more monstrous and cruel than this traffic," better organized than the equivalent trade in Tanganyika, "had happened in history." Was Petherick ever involved in this clandestine traffic? As a public official and a merchant, he would have had the opportunity. And the charges that cropped up in high places are difficult to discount altogether. But perhaps he fell victim to the toxic environment of rumor and recrimination around him. If he ever did participate in the trade, it was almost surely before his mission to meet Speke and Grant. What is beyond question, however: Speke was not the only one to accuse Petherick of being a slaver, and he did not single-handedly bring him to ruin.[12]

Then we arrive at the role played by, as he would come to be known, "Baker of the Nile," another official hero in the scramble for the great river. Might Baker have poisoned Speke's mind against Petherick in their days together at Gondokoro while the Pethericks were on their way? What do we know of the circumstances? That Baker was aware of the charges against Petherick and was at pains to say so in the letter he wrote him from Gondokoro; that Kate Petherick regarded him, not just Speke, as wishing Petherick ill; that Petherick believed a false report of his own death had "induced Mr. Baker to undertake this expedition" in the first place; that Baker had Speke and Grant to himself for five days before the Pethericks arrived; and that Baker had serious ambitions of his own. When the Royal Geographical Society asked him to help search for Speke and Grant, it was an arrangement of convenience: the Bakers were already in Khartoum, and what they were after was the Nile. In *The Albert N'yanza: Great Basin of the Nile and Explorations of the Nile Sources* (1866), Baker narrates the adventures and travails that ended, quite ecstatically for him, with the sighting of the falls that he named for Murchison and of the lake, another feeder of the Nile, that he named Lake Albert after the late Prince Consort. He also recounts what happened when Speke and Grant showed up in Gondokoro.[13]

At first, Baker exults at what the explorers have achieved: "hurrah for old England!! they had come from the Victoria N'yanza, from which the Nile springs. . . . The mystery of ages solved." But his feelings have an edge to them: "With my pleasure of meeting them is the one disappointment, that I had not met them farther on the road in my search for them." And, a little later, "I had been much disheartened at the idea that the great work was accomplished, and that nothing remained for exploration." Baker even says he asked Speke, plaintively: " 'Does not one leaf of the laurel remain for me?' " There did, the lake known as Luta N'zige, later to become Lake Albert, a prize that Speke effectively handed over to the Bakers for their own: "Both Speke and Grant attached great importance to this lake Luta N'zige, and the former was much annoyed that it had been impossible for them to carry out the exploration." The Bakers are Speke's heirs. That is why Baker became, in due course, "Baker of the Nile."[14]

The Albert N'yanza is grandly dedicated to the Queen: "To her Most Gracious Majesty / The Queen / I dedicate, with her permission, / This book / Containing the story of the discovery of the great lake / From which the Nile ultimately flows, / And which, / As connected so intimately, / As a Nile source, with the Victoria Lake, / I have ventured to name / 'The Albert N'yanza,' / In memory of the late illustrious and lamented / Prince Consort." Baker milks every drop he can from his achievement, even managing to suggest that he has found *the* source of the Nile, the lake from which it "ultimately" flows, though without depriving Speke and Grant of their precedence. In the ferociously competitive annals of exploration, Baker's dedication to Victoria is a minor extravaganza of possessive rhetoric. His preface goes on in the same self-celebratory way: "The work has now been accomplished. Three English parties, and only three"—Baker is setting aside any claim that might be made on Petherick's behalf—"have at various periods started upon this obscure mission: each has gained its end." This company of explorer-heroes includes the Scotsman, James Bruce, who travelled in Abyssinia towards the end of the eighteenth century; Speke and Grant; and now Baker himself: "Bruce won the source of the Blue Nile; Speke and Grant won the Victoria source of the great White Nile; and I have been permitted to succeed in completing the Nile Sources by the great reservoir of the equatorial waters, the Albert N'yanza, from which the river issues as the entire White Nile." If Bruce and Speke and Grant and Baker were winners, Petherick was decidedly the loser. Baker's huffing and puffing is the exuberance of someone who knows it took some good luck to achieve what he did.[15]

His ambitions, that is, gave him a motive for cozying up to Speke. We can assume he would have mentioned the rumors of Petherick's slave trading, and possibly have reported them as fact; after all, Petherick was away somewhere unknown and might have been up to almost anything for all Speke knew. If Baker could no longer look forward to sole possession of the Nile, he could at least associate himself with those who had gained the prize and learn whether any leaf of the laurel was left for him. Cutting Petherick out meant cutting himself in. It need not even have been Baker's explicit intention to subvert Speke, merely the fortuitous combination of his own ambition, Petherick's tarnished reputation, and Speke's impetuous nature: anyone who blows away a partridge running on the ground in a moment of aggravation cannot be counted on to react deliberately. However it happened, Baker must have been very happy when Speke threw in his lot not with Petherick but with him.

But whatever Baker may or may not have said, may or may not have done, he could not be held responsible for Speke's intemperate denunciations of Petherick once he returned to England. Nor could the very human tendency to treat badly those we have harmed in itself explain Speke's performance. If we are to believe Murchison about Speke's "visions"—and there is no reason not to—we can only assume that something very disturbing in kind, and quite opaque in its origins, had taken place.

Yet, antagonistic as he may have been and hysterical as he may have become, Speke nonetheless wrote Petherick a letter from Khartoum after their parting at Gondokoro that gave no hint of any difficulty between them. In fact, quite the contrary:

> We came down the Nile all right . . . and have lived ever since very comfortably under the tender care of your fair Fatma [the Pethericks' housekeeper]. To-morrow we hope to be well away in the early morning, consigning your small passages to their destination in as good order as you gave them to us. . . . I was sorry to find, on arrival here, that the townspeople had reported you dead, and in consequence of it the Royal Geographical Society had determined on sending the second thousand pounds to Baker, with a view to assist him in looking after us. . . .

The letter, essentially a polite thank-you note, goes on in this same helpful, if almost surrealistic, vein:

> To make the best of the matter, and to do justice to all, I wrote home a full explanation of our conversation at home before we left England, and the position in which we met at Gondokoro.
>
> Should you feel inclined to write a full statement of the difficulties you had to contend with in going up the White Nile, it would be a great relief to the mind of every person connected with the succouring funds, and also to myself, as the peoples' tongues are always busy in this meddling world.

After this apology, as it somewhat obscurely seems to be, for what happened at Gondokoro, Speke concludes with hearty good wishes, as if it had all been a house party weekend in the country: "With Grant's best wishes, conjointly with my own, to Mrs. Petherick and yourself, for your health and safety in the far interior, Believe me, Yours truly, J. H. Speke."[16]

No wonder that Murchison, writing to Grant in May 1864, was baffled. On the one hand, he had just received "a most *violent*" telegram denouncing Petherick from Speke in Paris. On the other, he knew of Speke's letter to Petherick from Khartoum, which he called, rightly enough, "*very* friendly." The two sides of Speke's divided personality seemed quite incompatible with each other.[17]

Yet, as Murchison would not have known, this extravagant dividedness equally marked his dealings with Sumunter and with Burton. Between the aggressive side of his nature, on the one hand, and the passively polite, on the other, there was a dramatic disconnect. As the story neared its end, irrational aggression won out. The hapless Petherick was the victim.[18]

"The Tail"

If Speke behaved strangely, even hysterically, when he denounced Petherick to Murchison in the spring of 1864, his manuscript corrections to *What Led* . . . , in the volume he sent to Simpson only months later in August, are quietly routine. The calmness that marks these corrections, almost without exception, matches the calmness in his account of why Burton stayed behind in Aden. Here Speke is just another author going about his normal business; at his writing desk, Petherick's wild-eyed antagonist becomes a different creature.[19] A look at these emendations will bring us back to the eight pages that were added to the three copies of *What Led* . . . , pages that would most likely have come into public view in autumn 1864 had Speke not died in September.

His attentions to detail extend even to such minor matters as page headings: "Feeders of the N'yanza" is changed to "First Sight of the N'yanza"; "Northward Extent of the Lake" to "Extent of the Lake"; "Missionary Prospects" to "Missionary and Merchant Prospects." Emendations in the text are, as a rule, equally small change: a hill-range "about 180 miles long and 20 or more broad" becomes a hill-range of "about twenty miles"; "water in the nullah extended upwards of half a mile" becomes "water in the nullah at this season only . . ."; "shooting hippopotami" becomes simply "shooting"—perhaps Speke grew sensitive about his reputation for slaughtering fauna. Only on two occasions does Burton appear in the emendations. First, in a footnote, Speke makes known that a cheque from Burton, supposedly drawn from "public funds" and intended to defray costs of Speke's passage to Africa, had not only never been credited to his account but had not "been debited to Captain Burton," something Speke must have been at some pains to learn; we are no doubt to think Burton appropriated the money. Second, in an emendation "written with pencil digging into paper," Speke substitutes "Captain Burton has supposed" for "some people have supposed;" at issue is a geographical disagreement about the Mountains of the Moon. The pencil digging into the paper is rare evidence of Speke's emotions stirring beneath the placid surface.[20]

But the emendations count for little beside the eight extra pages and the startling claim that Burton, not intending to return to England for many months, was planning a journey to Jerusalem instead. What can the circumstances of these eight pages have been? On the one hand, what is their bibliographic story? On the other, what is their human story? The bibliographic story is essential though not conclusive as to the motives that may lie behind it. Nor (of course) can it tell us whether Speke's account of Burton's plans is true.

For the bibliographic story, I rely on the expert knowledge of Nicolas Barker. That Speke had a second edition in his sights is evident from the letter to Simpson: "I have read through 'What led' and have made some corrections as you will see by the Vol. Sent. When the Second Edition comes out I wish you would attend to them please, and then return my copy." This much is straightforward. From here on, conjecture takes

over—though conjecture will be strengthened by an unexpected precedent in the publication history of Speke's earlier *Journal of the Discovery
of the Source of the Nile.*

This is what, bibliographically, can be inferred: that the eight extra
pages, continuously paginated and in the same format, were set at the
same time as the rest of the book; that a final, sixteen page section was
"cut short" while the book was being made up, the text ending on page
371 (followed by a small-type appendix running over to page 372, thus
creating a final four page section, signed 2A on page 369); that pages
373–80, appended as we now know to at least three copies of the text,
were then made up as an eight page section; that this section consists
probably of "imposed" page proofs—that is, proofs cut and folded into
consecutive pages; and, finally, that the original intention may have
been to continue the text for four pages more. It follows then that the
first mystery of the coda lies in the abridgement of the original text.
Why did this happen? Almost certainly it was through the influence of
the publisher, Blackwoods. For something remarkably similar had oc-
curred not many months before while Speke's *Journal of the Discovery of
the Source of the Nile* was in press. In that volume, too, the tail had been
cut from the body.

The full bibliographic story of *What Led . . . ,* if it is anywhere to be
found, probably lies in the Blackwoods archives in the National Library
of Scotland—from which the related story of the *Journal of the Discovery of the Source of the Nile* has been unearthed and studied, with differing conclusions, by Laurence Oliphant's biographer Anne Taylor and by
David Finkelstein, an historian of the publishing house and of its role in
editing and preparing the *Journal* for publication. When he encoun-
tered Speke's writing first, John Blackwood was appalled: he called it
"*abominable, childish,* unintelligible," and cutting the tail off the *Journal*
was the final act in a long, thorough, elaborate process of shaping the
narrative to make it a saleable commodity. The story of the *Journal* and

its tail, even though variously told by Taylor and by Finkelstein, pertains analogously to that of *What Led* . . . .[21]

According to Finkelstein, the lopping of the tail was merely to abbreviate a diffuse text that, even when published, ran to more than 600 pages. Nothing of special consequence, he reports, was in the deleted section; it was "merely a straightforward journal account of Speke and Grant's journey back down the River Nile . . . ." According to Taylor, on the contrary, the deleted section in fact "accused Burton of incompetence, cowardice, malice, and jealousy on their expedition of 1857–9." Speke then insisted, again according to Taylor, that if the tail had to be cut, it should nonetheless be printed for his family, a prospect that "terrified" the Blackwoods, John and William III, because they feared the accusations might become public. If this account is accurate, the bibliographic story of the *Journal* coincides very closely with that of *What Led* . . . .[22]

We might invent a scenario. Say that Speke hands Blackwood the manuscript of *What Led* . . . , including the tail. The publishers grow anxious once again, fearing lest Burton take legal action and heeding the reluctance of Georgina, the family matriarch, to engage in a public squabble—but they agree, having learned by experience that Speke was not easy to manage, both to print the eight pages and bind them into copies for Speke and his family. Still anxious that the eight pages find their way to the world beyond "Jordans," Speke starts work on corrections for a second edition, taking pains to be meticulous. He also consults the ladies, finds them agreeable or says he does and, knowing that the Blackwoods know that Georgina's opinion matters, tells Simpson: "The ladies all like the tail and with myself cannot see what more harm it could do than other parts contained in the body of the work, whilst all equally say the best policy is . . . 'speak the truth, and shame the Devil.'" This scenario is persuasive. But was Speke telling the truth about Burton's intention to travel to Jerusalem?

Jerusalem is not an unlikely place for Burton, with his attraction to holy cities—Mecca, Medina, Harar, Salt Lake—to have wished to visit.[23] Yet those to whom Burton is a hero will not be likely to believe Speke. Those who distrust Burton will be readier to think that Speke is telling the truth. Is there any way to explain the conflicting accounts? Might Burton have said he intended to go to Jerusalem and then changed his mind, realizing that he would be putting in jeopardy his stake in central Africa? Might he have said he was going to Jerusalem merely to account for his not travelling home with Speke, whose company he was thoroughly tired of? Surely he could have obtained from his friend Steinhaueser the medical certificate he needed—he explains in "Captain Speke" that "my companion's sick certificate was en règle, whilst mine was not"—if he had really wanted it; presumably he had a certificate in hand two weeks later. Or might Burton have lied, saying he intended to go to Jerusalem, planning in fact to take the next boat to London and hoping he could beat Speke to the Royal Geographical Society himself while his companion was in Somerset? Any of these possibilities would mean Speke told the truth as he knew it. Still there is little choice in the long run but to pick sides in the absence of convincing evidence one way or another—or at least to gauge the possibilities.[24]

What might be said for and against Speke? For and against Burton? And who is least likely—or more likely—to have lied or twisted the truth? On Speke's behalf, the very specificity of his claim that Burton intended to go to Jerusalem carries conviction, as do the casual fashion in which the claim is made and the equally casual proposition, in the letter to Simpson, that the ladies approve and agree, since little more harm can be done, that time has come to shame the devil. It all has an atmosphere of the "simplicity and almost childish innocence" that John Blackwood, a sharp observer, attributed to Speke—as, for that matter, did Burton. At the same time, Blackwood saw in him not only childish innocence but "the most wonderful shrewdness in his own particular way." It would have taken extraordinary shrewdness masquerading as innocence to invent the claim that Burton was going to Jerusalem and then present it with such perfect aplomb. Extraordinary but not impossible.[25]

But if Speke's claim is true, it follows that Burton was three times a liar who elaborated his story at each stage until it flowered into the famous dialogue that, it now turns out, may have never taken place at all. He certainly could have manufactured such a dogged lie, inventive as he was, and a letter in the archive of the Royal Geographical Society, unearthed by the Society's historian, Ian Cameron, suggests he may actually have done so: "a couple of days after Speke sailed for England," Cameron reports, "Burton wrote to the Society expressly to tell them that 'Captain Speke will lay before you his map explorations . . . and there are reasons for believing it [Speke's Lake Victoria] to be the source of the principal feeder of the White Nile.'" Yet even this evidence, both important and neglected, is not perfectly conclusive, for it does not exclude the possibility that Speke made an undertaking to Burton that he would not lose his share in any spoils.[26]

It remains almost as difficult to disbelieve Burton wholly as to disbelieve the apparent open-eyed innocence of Speke. Certainly the outraged Burton, scribbling angry marginalia in Speke's *What Led . . .* , was reacting spontaneously, not currying public favor. At the same time his anger was not necessarily tied to the fact of having been betrayed; anger might have inspired invention of the story. The pendulum swings back and forth. We have seen far less shrewdness in Speke than simplicity: his wholehearted commitment to his mother; his almost servile deference to his superior officers; his need, on the one hand, to seem to be in charge while not wanting, on the other, to breach the conventions of politeness and fellowship; his almost feverish dedication to slaughtering animals of every sort. These are marks of a not-quite-grown-up boy. So, in a different way, are the tantrums, amounting to hysteria, that Petherick and Burton inspired in him, not usually in public settings but in communications with family and friends, with whom we can assume he felt secure. When forced against the wall of necessity—that of coming to a conclusion—I usually find it harder to disbelieve Speke than Burton. Occasionally, it is the other way around. The scales are in almost perfect balance.

Speke's Death

Was it an accident or a suicide?

On September 15, 1864, Speke and Burton found themselves together on the platform at Bath where they were to debate the next day under the auspices of the British Association for the Advancement of Science. Not only would Speke have been nervous about the debate, he would have felt in Burton a dangerous and alien presence in the Somerset landscape. This was Speke country. The family seat was in Ilminster, only forty miles from Bath, and generations of the family were buried in the nearby parish church of Dowlish Wake, where Speke's younger brother Benjamin was rector. His older brother William lived in Corsham, some ten miles from Bath. His uncle-in-law, John Bird Fuller, lived in Neston Park, also near Bath. Burton—along with the British Association—had invaded Speke's own provincial world.

Isabel Burton tells what happened on the platform at Bath. It is almost as familiar now from repetition as the parting dialogue that Burton reported, or invented, between Speke and himself. "The first day"—September 15—"we went on the platform close to Speke. He looked at Richard, and at me, and we at him. I shall never forget his face. It was full of sorrow, of yearning, and perplexity. Then he seemed to turn to stone." This snapshot, coming soon after Isabel's description of Speke's speech at Taunton the previous December as "unequalled" for "vaingloriousness and bad taste" turns him in a flash from vainglorious braggart to sufferer, a man of sorrows—and maybe a suicide, able to turn himself to stone.[27]

There follows an emotional flood-tide, Speke's disaster engulfing all. "After a while he began to fidget a great deal, and exclaimed half aloud,

'Oh, I cannot stand this any longer.' He got up to go out. The man nearest him said, 'Shall you want your chair again, Sir? May I have it? Shall you come back?' and he answered, 'I hope not . . .' " As, of course, he did not. The next day, when Speke's "terrible accident" is announced, "Richard sank into a chair, and I saw by the workings of his face the terrible emotion he was controlling, and the shock he had received. When called upon to speak, in a voice that trembled, he spoke of other things and as briefly as he could. When we got home he wept long and bitterly, and I was for many a day trying to comfort him." Let us assume that this is all true. Such a torrent of feeling, stemming from Burton's belief when he heard the news that Speke had killed himself, could be regarded either as enmeshed with guilt or as the plain sorrow of someone who had endured many hardships with a companion who had now fallen by the wayside. In either case the deep currents running through the long, sad story break to the surface here at its close.[28]

It comes as no surprise to anyone who has followed Speke's life to find out what he did next, after the anxiety of seeing Burton at Bath: he set off to go shooting. As he fled the hall, maybe he thought back to the rush of "heated blood" that led him, in his anger at Sumunter ten years before, to blast away at the inoffensive partridge on the ground. Shooting was Speke's instinctive reaction to frustration or upset, a better sedative than alcohol or opium or sex. So, together with his cousin George Fuller and Daniel Davis, a gamekeeper, he set out to kill birds in Neston Park. No one could have predicted the strangeness of what happened next.

We know that Fuller and Davis were both at a distance from Speke when his gun fired, Davis as much as two hundred yards away marking birds, Fuller some sixty yards in front, gun probably at the ready. Neither, therefore, could have been totally sure of what happened. Whatever it was, it happened quickly and without warning, like any accident. While crossing a stone wall from one field to another, Speke seems to have propped his gun, the same gun as appears in his studio portrait from which the frontispiece of the *Journal* was engraved—a type without a safety, and half-cocked—on the wall; either that or he carried it over the wall, muzzle pointing upwards. When it went off, he was wounded mortally, at very close range, the charge passing through his lungs and destroying blood vessels above the heart. He said " 'Don't move me.' " A surgeon was called for, but Speke survived only fifteen minutes and was dead when the surgeon arrived. He was buried in the family vault in Dowlish Wake. Grant, Murchison, and David Livingstone, back in England between African sojourns, all attended the funeral.[29]

At a coroner's inquest, convened the day after the shooting, a jury "of respectable inhabitants" from Corsham took testimony from George Fuller, from the gamekeeper, and from the surgeon. Davis testified that the gun was a breech-loader without a safety—" 'but I should think the gun was quite safe and in the same state that Gentlemen's guns usually are.' " The jury determined that Speke's was an "accidental death," caused "by explosion of his own gun."

The verdict did not quiet speculation; the suspicion that Speke committed suicide had, and still has, almost irresistible appeal. Fawn Brodie believes suicide is "strongly suggested," adding that "it is now generally recognized that suicide is a supreme act of hate, often directed against someone one has loved." Hence "suicides are covered up, when at all possible, with elaborate fabrications designed to protect the living." George Fuller, "even if he was certain it was suicide, would have had strong motives to protect his distinguished relative's reputation, and also to conceal and thereby diminish his own sense of outrage." Brodie stops short of asserting deliberate suicide—but at very least, even if the death was an "accident," it was an accident on purpose: Speke's carelessness indicates "a strong preconscious inclination to suicide." That he in some way courted death was certainly true if in fact he came to Africa "to be killed." But that is not the same thing as saying he intended to kill himself as he climbed over a stone fence, gun at hand, in September

1864; nor even the same as to say that he wilfully exposed himself to risk.[30]

Mary Lovell's view seems at first to edge toward Brodie's: "Speke's connections insisted that his death was accidental. This is hardly surprising since suicide implied in his case cowardice." But taking into account the enormous awkwardness and unpredictable outcome of trying thus to kill oneself with a shotgun while going over a fence, Lovell decides finally, as if against her will, that Speke probably fell victim to an accident. She believes he was holding his gun by the muzzle rather than having recklessly placed it on the ground. And yet, in his studio portrait, the gun is also propped on the ground, facing upwards. Perhaps this was his habitual practice. Whatever the case, climbing a fence with a gun muzzle pointed anywhere near your heart, as Lovell comments, ignores all one has ever learned about handling guns. Speke was at best remarkably careless, probably distracted by and still remembering events in Bath.[31]

For any storyteller, suicide is more desirable as an outcome than accident. In Harrison's *Burton and Speke*, what would be more disappointing, after some hundreds of mettlesome pages, than to learn that Speke, failing to observe the most elementary precaution, dies of an accidental wound? The novelist makes the most of the hand he has been played:

> . . . Speke reloaded his weapon. His face began to twist in pain. . . . He felt a passionate emptiness.
>
> Sorry everyone.
>
> He stepped up on a low stone wall. His eye caught the shiny hieroglyph of a snail's path on the rock: a tiny river of slime.
>
> He held the barrel of the gun close to his side in a cold embrace. Neither Fuller nor Davis were watching; the sky wheeled and shimmered.
>
> When they heard the shot, both Fuller and Davis turned and saw their guest standing on the wall; he paused there, weaving slightly, then fell face forward into the field.

A suicide, surely, even if we are uncertain just what has happened. Or was it? "Many . . . assumed that Speke had killed himself, unable to face Burton, yet there were contrary and insistent reports: a hunting accident, nothing more . . . ."[32]

If it is in the interest of Burtonians and of novelists to believe Speke was a suicide, it is in the interest of his friends to believe he was not. Alexander Maitland thinks the death was accidental but reaches his verdict slowly, almost painfully: "it is the opinion of this writer after some four years' acquaintance with the facts, that Speke neither contemplated suicide, nor did he kill himself, and that his death was entirely accidental." I also believe it was accidental. But I would not be so certain of Speke's state of mind as to call it "entirely" an accident. Nor that it was just a hunting accident, "nothing more." It was an accident and something more—the kind of something about which, lacking any good way to speak, we are better off being silent.[33]

De Mortuis

Any student of the Victorian obituary, or the Victorian culture of death, could do worse than begin with Speke. The death of Prince Albert in 1861 ushered in a great age of public mourning, and Speke was almost a type of royalty in the public eye. Obituaries in the *London Times* and in *Blackwood's* spanned a range of mortuary styles, from the formal, moralizing, imperial—and first-page—notice in the *Times* to a florid and intimate notice by John Blackwood himself.

On September 19, the *Times* wrote at length about "the untimely death of Captain Speke." That it was accidental is taken for granted—and it is an occasion to moralize about the proper handling of guns: "Speke was, no doubt, a first-rate sportsman; but he paid the forfeit of his life for his momentary incaution in drawing his gun up towards him with the muzzles pointed to his body. While accounting for this accident, we would endeavour to make the example useful to save the lives

of others . . . [W]e would say any man who allows his companion to see
down his barrels ought to be sent out of the field, and any one who
finds himself able to look down his own barrels had better give up
shooting." Where we see mostly grim irony, the *Times* discerns a wholesome moral, uttered in the tones of a prim and knowing schoolmaster.

But the Nile is forever Speke's prize. In the obituary's last words: "In
all future time, Captain Speke, whose loss we deplore, must be remem-
bered as the discoverer of the source of the Nile." He is the model of an
eminent, exemplary Victorian, spreading the English gospel to the several corners of the earth: "We cannot but feel an interest in the fortunes
of that class of men among whom Speke was so eminent. They have
been in all ages our pioneers who have gone before our merchants, our
missionaries, our colonists, and have pointed out to us new regions
where we may make homes for the overflow of our populations, new
provinces for our great Empire, new countries adapted to the conditions required for the spread of our language, our institutions, and our
spirit of Anglo-Saxon freedom." This spells out mercilessly the colonial
and imperial agenda, and it is in good keeping with Speke's own conviction of Britain's civilizing mission. Yet, like Everest, the main appeal
of the Nile and its source was that it was there. A "gallant soldier," a
"sagacious and enterprising traveller," and a "bold adventurer," Speke is
a hero of his time as well as a missionary of empire.

After the moralizing prudence and imperial celebrating of the
Times—"be-careful-with-your-gun" and "three-cheers-for-empire"—
the woodnotes of John Blackwood in "The Death of Speke" sound a
wild lyricism from a distant northern land: "In the season when the
leaves change from green to brown, and are swept round and round by
the eerie autumn winds—when the summer purposes are ended, and
those of winter are not yet begun—in the midst of the customary
changes through which, year after year, we have all passed from summer
into winter,—the electric wires startle us with the astounding news that
the boldest explorer of the age has been killed in an English stubble-

field by the accidental discharge of a gun. The world stands in breath-
less awe at such an event." Dying in a mere English stubble-field is an
indignity unbefitting the boldest explorer of the age as well as a tragic
accident.[34]

The obituary is the natural home of the pious epithet: Speke once
again is a "tried" soldier, a "sagacious" discoverer, a "bold" explorer. But
the true skill of John Blackwood's notice lies in its conversion of liabilities, ones that he fully perceived, into assets. Speke's failure to have given
other African explorers—that is to say, Burton—their due is the case of a
plain speaker striving "to narrate what he himself did and saw" and
wanting to tell his story "plainly and frankly." And his failure to credit
those who turned the prose that Blackwood had once called "abominable" into something readable is the mark not of *amour-propre* but of
an unsophisticated author, "not sufficiently adroit in the craft of book-
making to be acquainted with the method of that form of pride that apes
humility," that is, the fake humility of specious acknowledgments that
"invariably . . . tend to uplift the glory of the author." We know that
Speke's war with Burton disturbed Blackwood. We can assume that his
failure to acknowledge the vast editorial help he received with the *Journal
of the Discovery of the Source of the Nile* did not really set well, either. In
death, however, Blackwood turns Speke's every limitation into a virtue.

In fact, Blackwood had found him a great puzzle in his impenetrable
mixture of childishness and shrewdness: "I never met with such a mixture of simplicity and almost childish ignorance, combined with the
most indefatigable energy and the most wonderful shrewdness in his
own particular way. It must have been this strange mixture of character
that carried him through, and gave him such power over these crea-
tures"—that is, the natives of Africa. But now, in death, childishness is a
divine innocence: "he realised that fine old idea of true chivalry, in
which the hero in the field becomes a lamb at home." And childishness
appeals to children, "the most sure judges of true goodness of nature,"
who "were delighted with him. He took to them, not with the patronis-

ing air of people doing the benevolent, but as one of themselves." We should all be so lucky as to have John Blackwood writing our obituary.[35]

Less calculated, and very touching, is the final tribute of Speke's *fidus Achates,* James Augustus Grant. While he was in the midst of transcribing the text of *A Walk Across Africa,* soon to be published in December 1864, Grant received word of Speke's death. Immediately he stopped work on his narrative to write about his friend and the fatal accident. In the published text of *A Walk Across Africa* almost three pages are devoted to Speke, edged in black, and incorporated as an interruption within the narrative, a vivid and visible intrusion of death in the routines of life. "Could he possibly be dead? Was there no hope? The telegraph gave us none." With his customary decency, Grant reproaches himself for not having joined Speke in Bath, as he had been asked to do: "had I gone thither and been with my friend, this calamity might have been averted." Then he eulogizes Speke in the same accents as John Blackwood, though without the same premeditation: "Captain Speke was, in private life, pure-minded, honourable, regardless of self, and equally self-denying, with a mind always aiming at great things, and above every littleness." Like Blackwood and Burton, Grant marvels at Speke's childlike ways: "He was gentle and pleasing in manner, with almost childlike simplicity, but at the same time extremely tenacious of purpose." With its "record of many happy days spent together," *A Walk Across Africa* is dedicated to Speke "affectionately and mournfully." And the friendship was inviolate: "it is now a melancholy satisfaction to think that not a shade of jealousy or distrust, or even ill-temper, ever came between us during our wanderings and intercourse." Not far offstage, by contrast, is Richard Burton, his name unspoken, his presence inescapable. If it would be good luck to have the adroit John Blackwood write one's obituary, it would be even better to have had the amiable James Augustus Grant as a friend.[36]

Meanwhile, Burton was not silent. And even if it is true that Isabel was long trying to comfort him, his distress did nothing to impede a

fierce post-mortem counter-attack. In November he delivered a paper
to the Royal Geographical Society incorporating his rebuttal to Speke's
claims. The next month he published an expanded version of the paper
as Part I of *The Nile Basin,* a volume that reprinted, as Part II, review essays of Speke's *Journal* from the *Morning Advertise*r by the octogenarian
Scottish geographer James M'Queen.[37] M'Queen's essays are pure vit-
riol. He serves Burton as a spear-bearer and the Pethericks, who had
sought his help, as their willing and eager counsel.

M'Queen's assault on the *Journal,* fierce on geographical matters, is
also fiercely and unpleasantly personal, the work of a cranky old man
who feels the threat of being proven wrong about the Nile, a subject he
had debated with Speke as early as 1859. "Towards the close of last summer," he begins, "Captain Speke, with true Oriental authority, announced that the source of the Nile was in the clouds, but forbade anyone to attempt to seek out the particular point until *Blackwood* had told
the world where that point was to be found." M'Queen's Speke is a
despot and a monster of ingratitude, "incautiously and spitefully" attacking Petherick and his "heroic and devoted wife." He is also a dupe.
When Rumanika, the king of Karagwe, asks Speke " 'whether or not the
moon made different faces, to laugh at us mortals on earth,' " M'Queen
lets a nasty imagination run free: "King Rumanika appears after all to be
a bit of a wag. . . . Let any one look at the moon when she is full, and
then say if she does not represent a photograph of Speke, back upper-
most, with both legs stretched out, and arms extended, grasping the
mountains of the Moon, [and] the Lake Nyanza. . . . In short the keen-
eyed Rumanika appears to have been laughing at Speke's credulity." This
is ugly caricature.[38]

But Speke's bizarre ethnographic investigations in Karagwe—along
with his sexual proclivities, a subtext of his man-in-the-mooniness—
give M'Queen a still better opening. The women of the Karagwe court
were extraordinarily large—on one page of the *Journal* the headline
reads "Wife-Fattening"—and Speke wanted to find out just how large.

Probably he thought he was following Burton's example, but the result is grotesque ethnographic-sexual comedy. Speke wrote: "After a long and amusing conversation with Rumanika in the morning, I called on one of his sisters-in-law," presumably with the king's consent. "She was another of those wonders of obesity, unable to stand excepting on all fours. I was desirous to obtain a good view of her, and actually to measure her, and induced her to give me facilities for doing so"—that is, to take off her clothing—"by offering in return to show her a bit of my naked legs and arms." It is hard not to suppose he may have offered her a view of something more than a bit of arm and leg. For enemies like M'Queen or the adept ethnographic investigator Richard Burton, the supposition must have been irresistibly attractive. Measure her various dimensions Speke did, even her height—a serious "engineering" problem because she can stand up only with the greatest difficulty. M'Queen's comment: "We believe none of our readers ever met with or heard of such a piece of 'engineering' as this, and we daresay will never wish to meet with such another." Fair enough.[39]

But this is not all. While the measuring has been going on, the woman's sixteen-year old daughter sits there "stark-naked before us," being duly fattened up by "sucking at a milk-pot, on which the father kept her at work by holding a rod in his hand." Speke then indulges in what he calls, with consummate naivete, "a bit of flirtation," inducing her "to rise and shake hands with me. Her features were lovely, but her body was round as a ball." Childish simplicity never played Speke worse. And when he says, as he does more than once, that he was lonely without a wife, M'Queen seizes another opening. To show that Speke had no need to be lonely and probably was not, M'Queen recounts the moment, at the court of King Mutesa of Uganda, when he is presented with an elderly woman " 'to carry my water' "—along with the king's vow that, if he did not think she was pretty enough, he could have his choice of ten others, "of 'all colours.' " Of this episode Speke says, with more caution than M'Queen attributes to him: "knowing full well that nothing so offends as rejecting an offer at once . . . , I kept her for the time being, intending in the morning to send her back with a string of blue beads on her neck . . . ." M'Queen omits Speke's intention to return the woman and entirely ignores his claim that the woman disappeared during the night, thus relieving him of his "anxieties." By enlisting the intemperate M'Queen in his quarrel and radically breaching the rule not to speak ill of the dead, Burton does no little harm to his own cause.[40]

In the aftermath of Speke's death, Burton is in fact more than ever a composite of conflicting selves. On the one hand, there is the grief-stricken figure weeping long and bitterly, being comforted by Isabel for many days; on the other, the vindictive antagonist who calls M'Queen's review "very able" and enlists him as a hit man in *The Nile Basin*—but nonetheless protests, even as he does so, that "I do not stand forth as an enemy of the departed," for "no man can better appreciate the noble qualities of energy, courage, and perseverance which he so eminently possessed, than I do." This doubleness, quite as pronounced as Speke's in different circumstances, evoked a puzzled comment from a reviewer in the *Morning Star,* December 28, 1864: "Captain Burton has made up for his own abstinence from rancour by disentombing Mr. M'Queen's merciless attack; but in doing this he has scarcely realised the magnanimous declaration of his preface."[41] One might ask the real Richard Burton to stand up, but we have grown used to the reality of fractured selves; and thus to the likelihood that Burton is simply being Burton. If anything is suspect, it is Isabel's account of his grief, for which we have no authority but hers, but such is the strangeness of the story and its protagonists that I suppose it is probably true, even if, or because, we cannot be certain for whom Burton weeps, or why.[42]

"Captain Speke"

In "Captain Speke," Burton's last published word on himself and Speke, he puts all his conflicting feelings on view. But finally, in the grand, romantic eulogy that brings the chapter to an end, he cauterizes the wounds that for a time outlasted even death.

"Captain Speke" begins curiously, with a teasing, even self-incriminating headnote from Lucan's *Pharsalia* that clothes the quarrel about the Nile in mock-heroic dress, in effect identifying Burton with Lucan's megalomaniac Caesar, who speaks to the sage Achoreus at Cleopatra's court:

> 'Tantus amor veri, nihil est quod noscere malim
> Quam fluvii causas per saecula tanta latentes,
> Ignotumque caput'—Lucan, X.189.

> ("Such [is] my love of truth that there is nothing I would rather learn than the causes of the river, lying hidden for so many ages, and its unknown source.")

If Burton is Caesar, Speke is Caesar's victim Pompey, the hero of Lucan's epic whose massive defeat at Pharsalus brought an end to the civil wars. Though he does not cite the lines that follow immediately, Burton has not forgotten them: "spes sit mihi certa videndi/ Niliacos fontes, bellum civile relinquam:" "If I had a sure hope of seeing the springs of the Nile, I would give up the civil war." The wry allusion comments on the strife between the latter-day combatants that had proven to be the death of one of them.[43]

Having opened on this note of ironic reconciliation, Burton repeats the words he had published eight years earlier in his preface to *The Nile Basin*: "I do not stand forth as the enemy of the departed. No man can better appreciate the noble qualities of energy, courage, and perseverance which he so eminently possessed, than do I." He regrets "the unfortunate rivalry respecting the Nile Sources [that] arose like the ghost of discord between us" and attributes its origin to "the jealousy and the ambition of 'friends' "—presumably Oliphant and perhaps Murchison also. Carefully and indeed winningly, Burton claims again "only the right of telling the truth and the whole truth, and of speaking as freely of another as I would be spoken of myself in my own biography."[44]

Especially compelling is Burton's comparison, in the context of events at Berbera, between French and English soldiery. It is nothing less than a comparison between Speke and Burton himself: "[Speke's] courage was of that cool order which characterizes the English rather than the French soldier." The "cool order" of English soldiery means to Burton not what we would usually think of as coolness but a habit of unconsidered recklessness: "The former, constitutionally strong-nerved and self-reliant, goes into action reckless of what may happen and unprepared for extremes: when he 'gets more than he bargains for' he is apt, like unimaginative men generally, to become demoralized. The Frenchman, with a weaker organization, prepares himself to accept the worst; and when the worst comes, he finds it, perhaps, not so bad as he expected." As a young boy, Burton lived in France, spent several years at school in Tours, ran with a gang of "small Anglo-French ruffians," perhaps even coming early to his nickname of "Ruffian Dick;" and when his family returned to England (Burton was ten), he and his siblings "were determined from the outset to dislike their native land." Now, years later, Burton tries to understand what has so divided him from Speke. Being English, Speke lacks imagination; Burton, being French at heart, has it to an extravagant degree. Probably Burton did in fact worry more than Speke, readying himself to expect the worst: "the devil drives." There could scarcely be a better insight into Burton's view of who he was—and who John Hanning Speke was—than the ancient antagonism between England and France. It is as if the destiny of the two men had been to act out the conflict and to embody, between them, the dark suspicions that lay on either side of the channel.[45]

Perhaps it was this insight into their difference that freed Burton from the grip of his antagonism. Nothing could be more handsome than his final eulogy: "Thus perished, in the flower of his years, at the early age of 37, by the merest and most unaccountable accident, an explorer of whom England had reason to be proud, and whose memory will not readily pass away. . . . With the active and intrepid energy, with the unusual temper, patience, and single-mindedness, with the earnest and indomitable pertinacity, and with the almost heroic determination, which he brought to bear upon everything that he attempted, the achievements of Capt. Speke's later life would doubtless, had his career run out its time, have thrown into the shade the exploits of his youth." Maybe, in the long run, one would like Burton to do one's obsequies.[46]

Was Speke a Cad?

Though Speke remains ever a puzzle, we can recognize what the puzzle consists of in his character with its mixture of childishness, simplicity, innocence, filial devotion, naivete, optimism, a desire to be liked, aspiration to leadership, susceptibility to influence, shrewdness, recklessness, impetuousness, and even an attraction to the romance of death. He could have been, though a second son, a West country-man if he had chosen to. But, in hindsight, the adventuring life seems his only imaginable destiny.

It is not hard to find reasons not to like Speke: his Anglo-Indian attitudes toward those with darker skin (which Burton handles rather more gently in "Captain Speke" than elsewhere: "he seemed to enjoy pleasure in saying unpleasant things—an Anglo-Indian peculiarity"); his love affair with the killing of beasts and birds; his speaking ill of Burton behind his back; his self-aggrandizing ways; his failure to credit others where credit was due; his strange vendetta against Petherick; his utter naivete in taking a tape measure to the arms, chest, thigh and calf of a naked African princess; and, if we were to believe Burton rather than Speke, his violation of a promise at a juncture that crucially and permanently affected both their lives—the allegation that has most wounded Speke's reputation. Yet we know now that we do not know well enough what took place in Aden to make a final judgment.[47]

And we have, as a counter-balance, the character witnessing of Blackwood and Grant: the one recognizing that to speak well of the dead, some gilding may be required; the other responding unreservedly to the death of a friend. We also have the witness of David Livingstone, whose presence at Speke's funeral implied his judgment of the participants in the great quarrel, even though he was unconvinced himself about the source of the Nile. Not only did he believe Burton had "behaved wickedly" by trying "to shut out every one else from his route to Tanganyika," he thought Burton's "atrocious attack on Speke after his death" should have "sunk him"—and failed to do so only because of his aristocratic backers. And even Burton, when he casts off the shackles of hatred, does not ask us to think Speke a cad. A boy at heart, with all that implies for better and for worse, Speke sticks in the mind with the pertinacity of other fallen heroes.[48]

CHAPTER SEVEN

Telling the Truth

Although historians are not always happy about it, it has become a commonplace that history does not give us things "as they really were" but, instead, an imaginative reconstruction of things as they might coherently claim to have been. Hayden White is an influential proponent of this view, one that he traces back to Hegel: "The historian has to interpret his materials in order to construct the moving pattern of images in which the form of the historical process is to be mirrored. And this because the historical record is both too full and too sparse." The historical record is too full in the sense that, in any historical account, some data are inevitably omitted. The record is too sparse in the sense that data capable of providing a fully satisfactory explanation of an event or circumstance are inevitably lacking. As a result: "A historical narrative is thus necessarily a mixture of adequately and inadequately explained events, a congeries of established and inferred facts, at once a representation that is an interpretation and an interpretation that passes for an explanation of the whole process mirrored in the narrative." This is a good description of what it is like in reconstructing the tale of Burton and Speke, in which the problems of the biographer—gauging individual motivations, making psychological inferences—are overlaid on those of every historian.[1]

W. H. Auden puts it provocatively: "History is, strictly speaking, the study of questions; the study of answers belongs to anthropology and sociology." Sociologists might agree; anthropologists might not. Historians might respond that the study of questions entails the possibility of answers, however various, that need to be treated. Creators of fiction, whose standard of truth is that of coherence, might say that questions are the reader's responsibility. Why (for example) does Isabel Archer marry Gilbert Osmond? Why does Hamlet so fatally delay? As for biographers, Leon Edel called them novelists under oath. Even so, a biographer cannot be required to swear to everything. That responsibility, and any awkwardness it entails, is a more reasonable demand on the forensic inquirer.[2]

Probabilities

These are among the questions, large and small, raised by the story of Burton and Speke:

1. What happened in Aden between Outram and Speke? Outram and Burton?

2. Who bore what responsibility for Speke's failure to locate the Wadi Nogal?

3. Did Speke actually say that he came to Africa "to be killed"?

4. Why did Burton (and Speke?) decide not to join the caravan leaving Berbera for Ogaden?

5. Did Burton bear indirect responsibility for the attack in Berbera? What happened during the early moments of the attack?

6. What part did Laurence Oliphant play in kindling antagonism between Speke and Burton? What was the nature of the friendship between Speke and Oliphant?

7. Did the sentiments that Burton found objectionable in Speke's Somali journal stem from Anglo-Indian racism?

8. Why did Burton ask Speke to join him on the expedition to seek the Nile?

9. What were the symptoms of cerebral impairment that Burton attributed to Speke?

10. Why did Burton allow, or enable, Speke to go by himself to the northern lake?

11. Did Baker influence Speke to turn on Petherick? Why did Speke attack Petherick so violently? Did Petherick ever engage in the slave trade?

12. Did Speke betray Burton after the expedition to the lakes? Does Speke or Burton more nearly tell the truth of their parting in Aden? Is there any way to reconcile the different accounts?

13. And was Speke's death an accident, no more, no less?

To these questions others might be added—but perhaps we need not inquire again whether Speke was all wet and bedraggled when he returned to camp after his unlucky mission on Lake Tanganyika.

Not all the questions admit the same degree of likelihood in their possible answers, and the kinds of evidence vary. Sometimes we simply have to take Burton's word or guess at some other reality behind it, as with his claim that Speke said he came to Africa to be killed. Sometimes the circumstantial evidence is slight, as with the question of Oliphant's influence: his review of *First Footsteps*, his presence on the *Furious*, even a trip to Paris that he took with Speke in 1864—these circumstances, involving association and proximity, entail no causal conclusions, though Isabel's belief in Oliphant's responsibility needs to be taken seriously. Sometimes circumstantial evidence is stronger, as with the question of Baker's influence: his knowledge of the charges against Petherick and his aspirations to the Nile add up to the fair possibility that he wanted to undermine Petherick and thus associate himself with Speke. Sometimes contrasting evidence can be weighed in the scales, as with the question of what happened in the attack in Berbera: Burton's account hangs together better than Speke's. Sometimes contrasting evidence, even when weighed in the scales, tips clearly in neither one direction nor the other, as with the conflicting stories of the parting in Aden. Sometimes an answer depends on putting one and one together and hoping that the answer is two: Burton objected to the "sentiments" expressed in Speke's journal and, as well, to his Anglo-Indian attitudes, making it plausible but not certain that the objectionable sentiments were those that expressed Anglo-Indian attitudes. Sometimes no inference can reasonably be made at all: how could we ever learn, one way or the other, whether Burton's prosecution of Sumunter generated hostility among the Somalis that led to their attack at Berbera? Curiously, the one question that has attracted the largest share of attention, whether Speke commited suicide, is also the one that may be answered with the highest degree of probability. Add to the coroner's verdict the difficulty and dubious outcome of attempting to kill yourself while climbing a fence with a shot from a gun propped against the fence or held by the barrel, and you end up with a probability approaching certainty that it was not an intentional suicide. Whether it was in some way a purposeful accident is another question, unanswerable because it depends on a knowledge, not to be had, of Speke's exact state of mind.

What to do in the presence of uncertainty? When the issue is less than crucial, normal practice for the biographer is to take a point of view—typically, that of the subject—and stick with it. In their naratives of the incident at Berbera, Farwell, Brodie, and Lovell all rely on Burton, but with differences. Farwell is most partisan: "Burton was awakened by a wild cry that the enemy was upon them. Leaping from his cot, he called for his sabre . . ." And, a little later: "As Speke stood hesitantly in front of the tent, he was hit by several stones from one side. He moved back under the fly"—whereupon Burton "snaps" at him: " 'Don't step back.' " Brodie is more tentative: Burton does not leap from his cot nor does Speke appear as hesitant; but, as in Farwell, he "move[s] back," which is to say, retreats, to the greater safety of the tent. Lovell is the most cautious of the three. Telling the story of Berbera on the first of two occasions, she omits Burton's "don't step back." Then, on a second telling, she gives Speke benefit of the doubt: "As the attack intensified, [Speke] was nearest the entrance; peering through the flaps, he must have inadvertently stepped back as the first rush came." This is generous in Burton's biographer, even though the claim that Speke "must have inadvertently stepped back"—like the claim that Burton was "undoubtedly" waiting in Berbera for family letters from home—is biographer's license, conjecture garbed as certitude. What Speke actually said of the critical moment was: "I . . . ran under lee of the fly of the tent to take a better survey. . . ."[3]

Alexander Maitland, as one would expect, tells the story much as Speke tells it, sometimes with highlights. He notices the implication, in Speke's bouncing out of bed, "that he was first in the fray"; describes Burton, as Speke had, as "fumbling with his revolver"; says that Speke "quickly dodged back" to the tent; and finally, when "enraged" by Burton's rebuke—Speke actually describes himself as "chagrined"—that he "ran forward into the gloom, firing at three men in rapid succession, dropping two of them." Biographers do not have the luxury, or the constraint, of forensic investigators, at least not often in their narratives. They have to tell their subject's story without hesitations at every twist and turn. Biographical narratives, like life, demand to be gotten on with. Exceeding some reasonable quotient of uncertainty risks narrative paralysis.[4]

But this has been a survey of evidence. Even an investigator cannot and need not introduce the issue of probability with every assertion, though a very high degree of probability, beyond reasonable doubt, is all that can be achieved. Often enough, probability claims can be taken for granted. But there are other moments when evidence is in conflict or assertion is plain guesswork. At such moments, there is no choice but to come clean. Coming clean means recourse to the vocabulary of the more-or-less probable, the likely, or the possible.

Using the necromancy of the "Find" command, I have measured (very roughly) the extent to which I have used this vocabulary in the preceding narrative. The numbers are high: "probably" occurs some thirty times; "perhaps," also more than thirty times; "likely" and "unlikely," taken together, another thirty; and there is much more than a scattering of other uncertainties: "possibly," "maybe," "I think," "may," "might." Half again as many instances may have fallen before the revisionary scythe. The vocabulary of the probable and the possible does not charm the eye or mind, and I have used it no more than seemed essential. The high count is a measure of how truly problematic is much of the evidence.

The merely probable is the chief end of neither fiction nor biography. Like fiction, biography aims to fix instability in a coherent and stable pattern. That is why the biographer, even under oath, will sometimes resort to a doubtful "undoubtedly." Biography may aim to make the coherent seem probable, but its truth and therefore its probability lie in other regions, that is, in the coherence of the story that it tells.

Concluding Unscientific Postscript

Here, in the end, come recollections of a beginning.

Forty years ago, I noticed something curious—unnoticed, I believed, by others—in Jonathan Swift's *Gulliver's Travels*. After Lemuel Gulliver's first, second, and fourth voyages (his third voyage is anomalous), all of them to very strange lands, the straight-faced, strait-laced Gulliver returns intent on demonstrating his veracity. Each time his evidence grows more tenuous, with increasingly less probative value. After his voyage to Lilliput, land of the very little people, he returns with tiny black cattle and sheep in his pockets and, with them, persuades the ship's captain who rescues him that he is not "raving." If he brings tiny animals home with him, he has been to a land where tiny animals exist.

After his visit to Brobdingnag, land of the very big people, he convinces his next rescuer that his brain is not "disturbed" because "truth always forceth its way into rational minds"; only as an afterthought does he lay in evidence such items, not necessarily probative, as a comb that he claims to be made with stumps of the Brobdingnagian king's beard and a collection of needles and pins "from a foot to half a yard long." Finally, after his last voyage to a land of rational horses, Gulliver's only evidence, less convincing still than "needles" and "pins," is his clothing, made from the skins of exotic animals and his shoes, made (he says) of dried Yahoo skins. Under these circumstances, proof of his truth-telling now depends altogether on the consistency of his tale: the captain, "after many endeavours to catch me tripping in some part of my story, at last began to have a better opinion of my veracity." While *Gulliver's Travels* had always been recognized as a satire on the lies of travellers, I thought (and still do) that I had stumbled on something new: that Swift's famous satire was a consideration of the nature and criteria of truth. I even constructed a theory of his intentions: perhaps, I thought, he was satirizing John Locke, whose theory of truth relied more directly on the coherence of propositions than their correspondence to things as they were in the world. Finding myself now in the company of Burton and Speke, wrapped in the tangled questions of their truths and their falsehoods, is (for me) something like a return to the start.[5]

Until the shrinking of the planet and the disapearance of frontiers—and the invention of photography, as well—strange tales of adventures in distant lands could be spun with comparative impunity: who was there to assess their truth or falsehood?[6] Remote lands were havens of body and mind, inaccessible to prying eyes, fertile soil for the vagrant imagination. And the aura of authenticity was in effect guaranteed by the presumption that tales were based on the traveller's journal, an on-the-spot record of what in fact took place. No one, after all, would be thought likely to fabricate a journal. And we all want others to believe that entries in the journal of our lives are true. Remoteness of place and time, paradoxically, helped ensure authenticity and authenticity helped ensure acceptance.

Yet even journals, from the very moment of inception, are subject to hazards of memory and perception, and over time, memory and its fallibilities take command. Events recorded on the spot may be questioned in retrospect; omissions, filled in. Nothing recorded "as it happens" can be synchronous with the events themselves—a truth on which the narrative of Sterne's *Tristram Shandy* is often wittily founded. Imagine, one last time, the Somali attack at Berbera. Suddenly, everything is chaos. Then, when the battle ends and they have been rescued, Burton and Speke record their separate versions of the story. Or maybe Burton only takes up his pen right away, for Speke was a less diligent journal-keeper. In any case, neither one of them can be supposed to have recorded what happened with absolute, sequential accuracy. Each no doubt remembers events to his own advantage. While Burton's admonition, "don't step back," stands out in Speke's mind, Burton himself may well have forgotten it. Perhaps he did not remember it even when reminded and had then to accept what Speke told him. The more one scrapes away at the evidence, the more the hopes of faithful reconstruction recede.

Burton knew the difficulties of reconstructing the factual—as Speke did not. He meditates on the subject, and on the differences between himself and his companion, in "Captain Speke." The context is Speke's unhappiness, divulged only after the passing of time, with Burton's appropriation of his Somali journal and his specimens of natural history:

> My companion had a peculiarity more rarely noticed in the Englishman than in the Hibernian and in the Teuton—a habit of secreting thoughts and reminiscences till brought to light by a sudden impulse. He would brood, perhaps for years, over a chance word, which a single outspoken sentence of explanation could have satisfactorily settled. The inevitable result was the exaggeration of fact into fiction, the distortion of the true to the false. Let any man, after long musing about, or frequent repetition of, a story or an ad-

venture, consult his original notes upon the matter, and if they do not startle him, I shall hold him to be an exception. And if he keep no journal, and be withal somewhat hard of persuasion, he will firmly hold, in all honour and honesty, to the latest version, modified by lapse of time. I made this remark more than once to my companion, and he received it with an utter incredulity which clearly proved to me that his was a case in point.

Of course it is Speke above all who is "hard of persuasion" (and who was at best a middling sort of journal-keeper); but when it came to the Nile, Burton was more than equally hard of persuasion—and equally accustomed, too, to muse about and repeat adventures and stories, including that of Speke's "betrayal." Here, smuggled into Burton's valedictory memoir of his companion, is the very story of their story together, its vexations and, for the eager teller of the tale, its insurmountable uncertainties. Here also is a good recapitulation of who these travellers were: the one, a complicated Englishman who renounced being English and saw into the complicated nature of truth; the other, a complicated Englishman, English to the end, who thought that truth was plain and uncomplicated—that what was true, was simply true. Some of the lasting sadness and strangeness of their story lies here.[7]

Notes

Notes

Chapter 2: The Odd Couple

1. In addition to Isabel's *Life*, I have consulted the following biographies of Burton, all published in recent decades: Edwardes (1963); Farwell (1963); Brodie (1967); Hastings (1978); McLynn (1990); Rice (1990); and Lovell (1998). Burne (1985) concentrates on Burton as a writer and also provides an abbreviated biographical sketch.

2. It would be doing Burton no favor to produce examples. To anyone seeking evidence, I would suggest looking at his translation of Catullus, published posthumously (1894).

3. *WL*, 15n.

4. Moorehead, 28; *WL*, 4; "CS," 2, 373.

Chapter 3: The Story Begins: Aden

1. Some have questioned whether the report was ever written, no copy having survived (Jutzi, 129).

2. Lovell, 151; Maitland, 7, 10.

3. *WL*, 5.

4. *WL*, 4, 21; "CS," 2, 379.

5. *WL*, 21n.

6. "CS," 2, 380, 381, 378; Maitland, 103.

7. *The Unfortunate Traveller* is not in the portion of Burton's library that survives at the Henry E. Huntington Library. His collection of fiction was sold in Trieste after his death. Many volumes also went missing over the years.

8. "CS," 2, 381. I am not confident that I understand Burton here.
9. "CS," 2, 381, 381–82.
10. "CS," 2, 382.
11. "CS," 2, 382; Maitland, 10.

Chapter 4: Somaliland

1. They were Lieut. Charles Cruttenden of the Indian Navy and the French explorer Charles Guillain (later a colonial administrator).
2. *FF*, 2, 95.
3. *Blackwood's* (May 1860), 561, in a prefatory letter to John Blackwood.
4. *Blackwood's* (June 1860), 683; cf. *WL*, 81, 82.
5. *FF*, 1, xxv, 2, 109; Brodie, 15.
6. "CS," 2, 383; Pelly, 13. But Pelly did not much enjoy the picture of himself and his party as Arabs: "we looked much the sort of company that Falstaff would have objected to marching through Coventry with."
7. "CS," 2, 383.
8. *WL*, 49.
9. *WL*, 49–51.
10. *WL*, 51, 51–52.
11. *WL*, 92–93.
12. *WL*, 93.
13. *WL*, 104, 109.
14. *WL*, 109, 112. Burton's marginal comment in his copy of *WL*: "not a word true" (Kirkpatrick, #1680, 112). This is one among Burton's many and dismissive marginalia in Speke's texts. Among them, typically: "rot"; "blarney"; "stuff"; "much *he* knows"; "no"; and, often, a single exclamation mark.
15. Cited in *FF*, 2, 72.
16. For an account of Coghlan's investigation of the Berbera incident, see Waterfield, 260ff.
17. *FF*, 2, 98; Waterfield, 262; *FF*, 2, 97–98.
18. Farwell, 122; Brodie, 122; Lovell, 172.
19. *FF*, 2, 98.
20. *WL*, 127. See below, pp. 63–65.
21. "CS," 2, 386; *WL*, 129, 130.
22. *WL*, 130.
23. *WL*, 130, 131.

24. In his copy of *WL*, Burton wrote in the margin: "Could not speak a word" (Kirkpatrick, #1680, 133).

25. *WL*, 133–34, 139; *FF*, 2, 104, 102; "CS," 2, 387.

26. *WL*, 132; "CS," 2, 386.

27. "CS," 2, 386.

28. "CS," 2, 384, 385.

29. For Oliphant's life, see Henderson; Taylor.

30. Henderson, 273; *Blackwood's* (October 1856), 499; "CS," 2, 384–85; Lovell, 220.

31. Lovell, 220; *WL*, 109n.

32. "CS," 2, 384; *FF*, 2, 112, 141, 144, 144–45.

33. In his edit, Burton transposes the information from December 4, the day Speke ascended the pass, to a lead-in summary of Somali geography, climate, and fauna. This sort of transposition further complicates any investigation.

34. *FF*, 2, 111; *WL*, 58.

35. *WL*, 57–58.

36. *FF*, 2, 124–25.

37. *WL*, 60–61, 61; *FF*, 2, 127.

38. Kirkpatrick, #1684, 2, 2.

39. *WL*, 62; *FF*, 2, 127–29.

40. *FF*, 2, 129.

41. *WL*, 64, 65.

42. *MSE*, 7; *WL*, 168; *Blackwood's* (September 1859), 344; *WL*, 210.

43. *Life*, 1, 309.

44. *WL*, 107, 108.

45. See Lovell, 40; also 438, quoting a letter from Murchison to Grant, May 1864, concerning Speke's "wild and impractical scheme of regimentizing niggers and proselytizing Africa on a new plan. . . ."

Chapter 5: Seeking the Nile

1. Edwardes, in his romanticized biography of Burton, proposes that "the 'strange' relationship of Burton with Speke . . . was an ill-fated homosexual affair" (xiii).

2. Lovell, 298, 221.

3. *LR*, 1, 385: "by his distances and directions we were enabled to lay down the Southern limits, and the general shape of the Nyanza . . ."

4. Ondaatje, 177.

5. Cf. Stafford, 168ff.

6. *LR*, 1, xiii; Stafford; *Journal*, 2.

7. *LR*, 1, xiv.

8. *LR*, 1, xiv, xiv–xv, xv; 5.

9. *LR*, 1, 71; 1, 179; 2, 85–86; 2, 461; 1, 169.

10. *LR*, 1, 214; 1, 215.

11. Lovell, 318, 319.

12. *LR*, 2, 290.

13. *LR*, 2, 91–92n; 2, 91–92.

14. After Lewis Pelly's expedition to Riyadh in 1865, he was unwilling to share any credit with his comrades and even prevented one of them from writing about it (Pelly, viii).

15. Kirkpatrick, #1680, 261; Lovell, 280.

16. *LR*, 2, 171; 2, 188; 2, 171.

17. *Blackwood's* (October 1859), 393; *WL*, 251.

18. Brodie, 335, 336; Lovell, xvi.

19. Quoted in Brodie, 185; Waterfield, 285–86.

20. *LR*, 2, 204; *WL*, 271.

21. *LR*, 2, 204; "CS," 2, 388–89.

22. *LR*, 2, 209.

23. See Finkelstein, " 'Unravelling Speke.' "

24. See below, pp. 92–98.

25. *Blackwood's* (September 1859), 357; cf. *WL*, 245.

26. *MSE*, 11; *WL*, 176.

27. *MSE*, 15–16; *WL*, 185.

28. *WL*, 250–51; *Blackwood's* (October 1859), 393; *WL*, 251.

29. Burton's marginal comment: "The Shaykh lied . . ." (Kirkpatrick, #1680, 261).

30. *Blackwood's* (October 1859), 396, 398; *WL*, 261n., 251.

31. Edwardes, Hastings, and McLynn also reproduce the conversation. Rice does not but cites other evidence from Burton. Burne, perhaps more sceptical, seems not to assume Speke's betrayal. A comparison of the many differing accounts, though it would be of interest as a study in biographical tactics, is not necessary here.

32. Farwell, 174.

33. Farwell, 175.

34. Brodie, 166.

35. Lovell, 293.

36. Maitland, 94.

37. *LR*, 1, xv; "CS," 2, 390; *Life*, 1, 327.

38. Harrison, 205; Penzer, 310; *Life*, 1, 258ff.

39. *Life*, 1, 327; Brodie, 355, n. 30.

40. Altick, 105.

41. *QKC*, 426.

42. Quoted in Brodie, 177; quoted in Maitland, 134, 135.

43. *WL*, Add., 373, 374, 374–75, 376, 378.

44. *WL*, Add., 379–80, 380. "Rigby" is General Christopher Palmer Rigby, the British consul in Zanzibar.

45. This passage is deleted, however, in the emendations that Speke sent to Simpson.

46. *WL*, Add., 380.

Chapter 6: Was Speke a Cad?

1. Farwell, 178; Brodie, 221; Maitland, 96; Taylor, 66.

2. Quoted in Lovell, 323; 328.

3. *QK*, 180, 181.

4. Lovell, 339.

5. Lovell, 338; Johnson, 314; Maitland, 115.

6. Petherick, 2, 127; 2, 127–28;

7. Petherick, 2, 19; 2, 20.

8. Petherick, 2, 139; 2, 139–40; 2, 140.

9. Lovell, 439; quoted in Lovell, 440.

10. Petherick, 2, 141.

11. Petherick, 2, 125; 2, 125–26; 2, 143; 2, 140.

12. Moorehead, 80, 81.

13. Petherick, 2, 132.

14. Baker, 1, 73; 1, 75; 1, 76; 1, 75.

15. Baker, 1, xxi.

16. Petherick, 2, 132–33.

17. Quoted in Lovell, 439.

18. Grant, 366ff., somewhat hesitantly defends, or at least excuses, Speke's resentment at Petherick's failure to meet them in Gondokoro. But he does not

believe Petherick traded in slaves; rather, he "tried to put down this illicit traffic" (371). Grant explains the decision to stay at Petherick's house in Khartoum as motivated by a decorous wish to "reside under [the] protection" of the British consulate (400).

19.   While I was contemplating these contradictions in Speke, there appeared in the *New York Times* sports section for January 20, 2005, an article about a professional football player, one of whose teammates said of him: " 'After I first met him, I thought he had a split personality. . . . He is the most gentle, cordial person you can meet off the field. And then he turns into this madman, this warrior, once he steps on the field' " (A, 26). Violent sports are one way humankind has found to delimit and contain the double feelings of which we probably all have some experience—and that seem to have bedeviled Speke to an extreme degree.

20.   I record again my obligation to Nicolas Barker, who has assembled information concerning the Keynes copy of *What Led* . . . , including the fact of Speke's pencil "digging into paper." I also record again my obligation to Dan Cook, who generously made the volume available.

21.   Quoted in Finkelstein, " 'Unravelling Speke,' " 45.

22.   Finkelstein, " 'Unravelling Speke,' " 57n.; Taylor, 111. Finkelstein calls Taylor's account hasty and erroneous. And, as edited, abbreviated ("by approximately two-thirds"), and printed in 1977 by Maitland, "Speke's Nile Diary," evidently the tail of the *Journal*, matches Finkelstein's description: it is straightforwardly journalistic. Burton is nowhere to be found (*Blackwood's* [May 1977], 371–85). Yet Taylor supports her account with what seems to be specific and careful evidence. How did two responsible scholars come up with such dramatically opposing versions of the same material? It is as if a curse hangs over reconstructions of the Burton-Speke story.

23.   As was pointed out to me by Dane Kennedy.

24.   "CS," 2, 390.

25.   Quoted in Finkelstein, *House of Blackwood*, 68.

26.   Quoted in Cameron, 81.

27.   *Life*, 1, 389; 388.

28.   *Life*, 1, 389.

29.   On Speke's death, see Maitland, 199–219; and Lovell, 443–58.

30.   Brodie, 226.

31.   Lovell, 449.

32.   Harrison, 409, 410.

33. Maitland, 217.
34. *Blackwood's* (October 1864), 514–16.
35. Quoted in Finkelstein, *House of Blackwood*, 68.
36. Grant, 347, 348, ix.
37. Variously spelled M'Queen, McQueen, MacQueen.
38. *NB*, 67, 71, 72, 101–2.
39. *Journal*, 209, 231; *NB*, 99.
40. *Journal*, 231, 309; *NB*, 107–8.
41. The review from the *Morning Star* is clipped and pasted on the inside back cover of Burton's copy of *The Nile Basin* (Kirkpatrick, #20).
42. *Life*, 1, 408; *NB*, 6.
43. "CS," 2, 371.
44. "CS," 2, 372.
45. "CS," 2, 386, 386–87, 387; Lovell, 7.
46. "CS," 2, 398–99.
47. "CS," 2, 388.
48. *QKC*, 388, lot # 436, a letter from Livingstone to Sir Thomas Maclear, May 27, 1865. Livingstone also says: " 'Burton is an awful ruffian—I must keep clear of his spoor....' "

Chapter 7: Telling the Truth

1. White, 51.
2. Auden, 97.
3. Farwell, 122, 123; Brodie, 123; Lovell, 174–75, 287; *WL*, 132.
4. Maitland, 36.
5. *GT*, 79, 145, 146, 276, 287; see Carnochan, pp. 116–65.
6. On the lying habits of travellers, fictional and otherwise, see Adams.
7. "CS," 2, 385–86.

Works Cited

Items marked with an asterisk are cited for reasons of accessibility, but citations have been checked against the original text.

Adams: Adams, Percy G. *Travelers and Travel Liars, 1660–1800.* Berkeley: U. of California Press, 1962.

Altick: Altick, Richard D. *The Scholar Adventurers.* New York: Macmillan, 1950.

Auden: Auden, W. H. *The Dyer's Hand and Other Essays.* New York: Random House, 1962.

Baker: Baker, Samuel White, Sir. *The Albert N'yanza, Great Basin of the Nile, and Explorations of the Nile Sources.* 2 vols. London: Sidgwick and Jackson, 1962. [1866]

Blackwood's: Blackwood's Edinburgh Magazine.

Brodie: Brodie, Fawn M. *The Devil Drives: A Life of Sir Richard Burton.* New York: W. W. Norton, 1967.

Burne: Burne, Glenn S. *Richard F. Burton.* Boston: Twayne Publishers, 1985.

Cameron: Cameron, Ian. *To the Farthest Ends of the Earth: 150 Years of World Exploration by the Royal Geographical Society.* New York: E. P. Dutton, 1980.

Carnochan: Carnochan, W. B. *Lemuel Gulliver's Mirror for Man.* Berkeley: U. of California Press, 1968.

"CS": Burton, Richard Francis, Sir. "Captain Speke," *Zanzibar: City, Island, and Coast.* 2 vols. New York: Johnson Reprint, 1967. [1872]*

Edwardes: Edwardes, Allen. *Death Rides a Camel: A Biography of Sir Richard Burton.* New York: The Julian Press, 1963.

FF: Burton, Richard Francis, Sir. *First Footsteps in East Africa; or, an Exploration of Harar.* Ed. Isabel Burton. 2 vols. London: Tylston and Edwards, 1894. (Memorial edition of *The Works of Captain Sir Richard F. Burton*, vols. 6–7). [1856]*

Farwell: Farwell, Byron. *Burton: A Biography of Sir Richard Francis Burton.* New York: Holt, Rinehart and Winston, 1963.

Finkelstein, " 'Unravelling Speke' ": Finkelstein, David. " 'Unravelling Speke': The Blackwoods and the Construction of John Hanning Speke as Author in His *Journal of the Discovery of the Source of the Nile*." *The Bibliotheck: A Scottish Journal of Bibliography and Allied Topics* 18 (1992–93), 40–57.

Finkelstein, *House of Blackwood*: Finkelstein, David. *The House of Blackwood: Author-Publisher Relations in the Victorian Era.* University Park: Pennsylvania State U. Press, 2002.

Grant: Grant, James Augustus. *A Walk Across Africa; or, Domestic Scenes from My Nile Journal.* Edinburgh and London: W. Blackwood and Sons, 1864.

GT: Swift, Jonathan. *Gulliver's Travels. The Prose Writings of Jonathan Swift*, Volume 11. Ed. Herbert Davis. Intro. Harold Williams. Oxford: Basil Blackwell, 1965.

Harrison: Harrison, William. *Burton and Speke.* New York: St. Martin's/Marek, 1982.

Hastings: Hastings, Michael. *Sir Richard Burton: A Biography.* New York: Coward, McCann & Geoghegan, 1978.

Henderson: Henderson, Philip. *The Life of Laurence Oliphant, Traveller, Diplomat, and Mystic.* London: R. Hale, 1956.

Johnson: Johnson, Samuel. "Idler 103." *The Idler and The Adventurer. The Yale Edition of the Works of Samuel Johnson*, Vol. 2. Ed. W. J. Bate et al. New Haven and London: Yale U. Press, 1963.

Journal: Speke, John Hanning. *Journal of the Discovery of the Source of the Nile.* Edinburgh and London: W. Blackwood and Sons, 1863.

Jutzi: *In Search of Sir Richard Burton: Papers from a Huntington Library Symposium.* Ed. Alan H. Jutzi. San Marino. Calif.: Huntington Library, 1993.

Kirkpatrick: *A Catalogue of the Library of Sir Richard Burton, K.C.M.G., Held by the Royal Anthropological Institute.* Ed. B. J. Kirkpatrick. London: Royal Anthropological Institute, 1978. Materials from the catalogue, identified here by entry number, are now held by the Henry E. Huntington Library.

LR: Burton, Richard Francis, Sir. *The Lake Regions of Central Africa: A Picture* *of Exploration.* 2 vols. Intro. Alan Moorehead. New York: Horizon Press, 1961. [1860] *

Life: Burton, Isabel, Lady. *The Life of Captain Sir Richard F. Burton.* 2 vols. Ed. W. H. Wilkins. London: Duckworth, 1898. [1893] *

Lovell: Lovell, Mary S. *A Rage to Live: A Biography of Richard and Isabel Burton.* New York: W. W. Norton, 1998.

McLynn: McLynn, Frank. *Burton: Snow upon the Desert.* London: John Murray, 1990.

Maitland: Maitland, Alexander. *Speke.* London: Constable, 1971.

Moorehead: Moorehead, Alan. *The White Nile.* New York: Harper, 1960.

MSE: Speke, John Hanning. *My Second Expedition to Eastern Intertropical Africa.* Cape Town: S. Solomon, 1860.

NB: Burton. Richard Francis, Sir, and James M'Queen. *The Nile Basin.* London: Tinsley Brothers, 1864.

Ondaatje: Ondaatje, Christopher. *Journey to the Source of the Nile.* Toronto: Harper Collins, 1998.

Pelly: Pelly, Lewis, Sir. *Report on a Journey to Riyadh in Central Arabia. 1865.* Intro. R. L. Bidwell. Cambridge, Eng. and New York: Oleander, 1978. [1865]

Penzer: Penzer, N. M. *An Annotated Bibliography of Sir Richard Francis Burton, K.C.M.G., by Norman M. Penzer.* Preface, F. Grenfell Baker. London: Dawson's of Pall Mall, 1967. [1923]

Petherick: Petherick, John. *Travels in Central Africa and Explorations of the Western Nile Tributaries. By Mr. and Mrs. Petherick.* 2 vols. London: Tinsley Brothers, 1869.

QK: The Search for the Source of the Nile: Correspondence between Captain Richard Burton, Captain John Speke and Others, from Burton's Unpublished East African Letter Book, Together with Other Related Letters and Papers in the Collection of Quentin Keynes, Esq., Now Printed for the First Time. Ed. Donald Young. Preface, Quentin Keynes. London: Roxburghe Club, 1999.

QKC: The Quentin Keynes Collection, Part I: Important Travel Books and Manuscripts, Wednesday 7 April 2004. London: Christie's, 2004.

Rice: Rice, Edward. *Captain Sir Richard Francis Burton: The Secret Agent Who Made the Pilgrimage to Mecca, Discovered the Kama Sutra, and Brought the Arabian Nights to the West.* New York: Scribner's, 1990.

Stafford: Stafford, Robert A. *Scientist of Empire: Sir Roderick Murchison, Scientific Exploration and Victorian Imperialism.* Cambridge, Eng.: Cambridge U. Press, 1989.

Taylor: Taylor, Anne. *Laurence Oliphant, 1829–1888*. Oxford: Oxford U. Press, 1982.

Waterfield: Burton, Richard Francis, Sir. *First Footsteps in East Africa*. Ed. and Intro. Gordon Waterfield. New York: Praeger, 1966.

White: White, Hayden. *Tropics of Discourse: Essays in Cultural Criticism*. Baltimore: Johns Hopkins U. Press, 1985. [1978]

WL: Speke, John Hanning. *What Led to the Discovery of the Source of the Nile*. Edinburgh and London: W. Blackwood and Sons, 1864.

WL, Add.: Speke, John Hanning. *What Led to the Discovery of the Source of the Nile*. Edinburgh and London: W. Blackwood and Sons, 1864. Pp. 373–80.

Index

In this index an "f" after a number indicates a separate reference on the next page, and an "ff" indicates separate references on the next two pages. A continuous discussion over two or more pages is indicated by a span of page numbers, e.g., "57–59."